THE POWER TO
PREVENT
SUICIDE

A Guide for
Teens Helping Teens

Richard E. Nelson, Ph.D., and Judith C. Galas

THE POWER TO
PREVENT
SUICIDE

A Guide for
Teens Helping Teens

Richard E. Nelson, Ph.D., and Judith C. Galas

Edited by Pamela Espeland

free spirit
PUBLiSHiNG®

Works
for kids™

Library of Congress Cataloging-in-Publication Data
Nelson, Richard E.
  The power to prevent suicide : a guide for teens helping teens / by Richard E. Nelson and Judith C. Galas.
      p.   cm.
  Includes bibliographical references and index.
  ISBN 0-915793-70-9
  1. Teenagers—United States—Suicidal behavior—Juvenile literature. 2. Suicide—United States—Prevention—Juvenile literature. [1. Suicide.] I. Galas, Judith C., 1946– . II. Title.
HV6546.N45 1994
362.2'87'0835—dc20   94-5594
                                                                            CIP
                                                                            AC

10 9 8 7 6 5 4
Printed in the United States of America

Cover and book design by MacLean & Tuminelly
Index compiled by Eileen Quam and Theresa Wolner

"How You Can Educate Others: A Step-by-Step Action Plan" in Chapter 9 is adapted from "10 Tips for Taking Social Action" in *Kids with Courage: True Stories about Young People Making a Difference* by Barbara A. Lewis (Free Spirit Publishing, 1992). Used with permission of the publisher.

Free Spirit Publishing Inc.
400 First Avenue North, Suite 616
Minneapolis, MN 55401-1730
(612) 338-2068

Dedication

To my family, most of all Barbara, for their love.
—REN
To Cindy, who's always there.
—JCG

Acknowledgments

The Power to Prevent Suicide grew out of the experiences and the problems of young people who have attempted or committed suicide. We thank their parents, counselors, friends, teachers, and principals for sharing those stories, and for making us believe that teaching teens about suicide can save young lives.

We also want to thank Free Spirit Publishing for believing in this book and Pamela Espeland for her thoughtful, intuitive, and creative editing.

CONTENTS

INTRODUCTION

Fourteen-year-old Jack Renfro* of Laredo, Texas, had been depressed ever since his brother's death in the spring. He thought a lot about killing himself. To him, it seemed better than going on living without his big brother.

Like many suicidal teens, Jack didn't keep his plan a secret. In fact, he told 21 friends just what he was going to do that October weekend in 1987. Those friends either didn't believe him or they didn't know what to do, because they did nothing. No one stopped Jack from putting on his best suit and tie, taking a gun from his house, going to his brother's grave, putting the gun to his head, and pulling the trigger. Jack was one of more than 5,000 young people who committed suicide that year.

Researchers have gathered a lot of data on teen suicide. They have learned that at least half of America's young people have thought about killing themselves.[1] Like Jack's thoughts, these thoughts are much more serious than the "I wish I were dead" kind we've all had when we were frustrated, embarrassed, angry, or sad.

Researchers estimate that each day more than 1,000 American teenagers attempt suicide, and 18 of them die.[2] Some of the research numbers tell us that if you're in a school with 2,000 students, about 500 of your classmates may be thinking about suicide, and 50 will attempt suicide each year.[3] Every four years, someone in your school will commit suicide.

The researchers also know that just like Jack, most young people share their suicidal thoughts with friends. In fact, when

....

*The stories in this book are real, but we have changed the names to protect people's privacy.

1

young people were asked, "Who would you tell about wanting to commit suicide?," 90 percent said they would tell a friend first.[4]

What would you do if a friend confided to you that he or she was going to commit suicide? Would you ask your friend to tell you about his or her sad feelings and plans to die? Would you go with him or her to an adult who would be able to help? Or would you think your friend was just kidding? Would you decide not to get involved because you believed your friend would snap out of it?

Jack didn't have to die. If only one of the many friends who spoke with him that weekend had told a teacher, coach, counselor, or parent what he was planning to do, he probably would be alive today. He'd still miss his brother, but he'd also be in the process of learning how to work past his pain to build a new life for himself.

You're an important key to helping stop young people like Jack from committing suicide. You probably know some teens who talk about committing suicide. You may even have thought about killing yourself, or you may have tried. We believe you can save a friend— or yourself—from committing suicide.

In fact, you might be able to do a better job of reaching your troubled friends than many of the adults around you. Your friends trust you. They know that you understand what it feels like to be a teen and the kinds of problems young people today have to struggle with. They can be themselves around you, and they might tell you things that they would never tell their parents or other adults. That puts you in a special position to make a difference and possibly even save someone's life.

The person whose life you save doesn't have to be your best friend. It might be someone you sit next to in one of your classes. It might be a friend you talk to a lot, or someone you just say "hi" to in the halls now and then. The point really isn't whether you're best friends or not. The point is, if you were in trouble, wouldn't you want someone to help you?

Why We Wrote This Book

Many books have been written about suicide in general and teen suicide in particular. You may have read some of them yourself. If so, you may be wondering why anyone would want to write or read another book on this topic.

The fact is, for whatever reason, other books don't seem to be working. Maybe not enough people are reading them. Maybe those books aren't saying what teens most want and need to know about suicide. All we know for certain is that the rate of teen suicide has increased dramatically in the past 20 years, and more young people are killing themselves today, right now, than ever before. You know this, too. You've read the stories in newspapers and magazines, and you've seen them on the news. One of those stories may have been about someone you knew personally—a friend, a classmate, or another teen in your school or neighborhood.

The statistics on suicide, and especially the experience of grieving someone's suicide, can be frightening and overwhelming. You may be feeling powerless, as if there's nothing you can do about the needless loss of life. But there *is* something you can do. And that's what this book is about.

The Power to Prevent Suicide recognizes the power you have to help your peers and yourself. In this book, we'll tell you what you can say and do to be a suicide preventer. We'll give you specific suggestions for reaching out, listening to, and helping someone who's thinking about suicide. We'll explain how young people like you can be the first line of defense against the rise in teen suicide. And we'll show how you, personally, can take positive, timely action to save a life.

We wrote this book because we believe that teenagers are capable enough to notice when someone may be suicidal, and caring enough to want to do something about it. We *didn't* write this book to make you a counselor. It takes many years of schooling and experience to become a counselor. But it doesn't take years of schooling and experience to be a caring person. All it takes is the desire to help someone who needs help.

We *didn't* write this book to diminish the important role parents and other adults can play in preventing suicide. But parents, like teens, often are uninformed about suicide. Parents, like teens, often are fearful of the word "suicide." And parents often don't know what to do when they are concerned about one of their own children.

Many parents have helped to prevent their children from killing themselves. These parents have seen the warning signs, and they have listened well. They have created homes where children and teens can openly talk about any problem. Teens who have parents like this are fortunate.

Many teens, however, feel that their parents don't understand them. They feel that they can't go to their parents when they are in trouble. Maybe their parents don't listen. Maybe they are preoccupied with their own problems. Or maybe they seem too "perfect." Sometimes it's hard for young people to believe that their parents ever had any serious problems when they were growing up, and it's easy to assume that parents don't understand the problems of teenagers today. These perceptions may be inaccurate, but they can still keep teens from going to their parents when they need help.

If you have parents who love you, who listen, who try to understand, who sincerely want to help, then they should be the *first* people you go to with questions about suicide or concerns that a friend may be considering suicide. But if you don't feel comfortable talking with your parents, please find another adult you like, respect, and trust.

You may decide to share this book with your parents or other adults. That would be great. Although we have written it especially for young people, we hope that adults will read it, too. We hope you will talk about it together. One big problem with suicide is that people don't want to talk about it. This book may be a way for you, your parents, your teachers, and other adults to bring this subject out into the open, where you can discuss it honestly and do something about it.

About This Book

We have divided this book into three parts.

- Part One, "Why, What, and Who," explores why someone might want to die, what you need to know about suicide and suicidal people, what warning signs to look for, and who's likely to be at risk.

- Part Two, "How to Be a Suicide Preventer," guides you through the steps of helping a troubled friend. You'll learn how to reach out, how to listen, and how to get help for your friend. We'll also tell you how to protect yourself against your own suicide and how to comfort yourself should someone you know and love attempt or commit suicide. After all that, we'll give you some ideas on how to get your community and school involved in saving young people's lives.

- In Part Three, "Resources," you'll find out about other books on suicide as well as crisis centers, community resources, and national organizations that can provide you with more information about suicide.

Before you start reading Part One, be sure to fill in the blanks on the form you'll find on page 8.* To help a friend who's thinking about suicide, you'll need to know where you can go for help. So write down the work and home phone numbers and addresses of the adults you trust the most. Then write down the phone number of your local crisis center. If and when you need this important information, you'll have it at hand.

Finally, there are a few words and phrases we use in specific ways throughout this book, and we want you to know what they mean before you start reading the chapters.

- When we use the term *suicidal,* we don't mean "depressed" or "sad." When we describe someone as suicidal, we mean "physically dangerous to himself or herself." People are said to be suicidal when their actions or ideas get fixed on suicide.

- An *attempted suicide* happens when someone tries to take his or her life but doesn't die. People who attempt suicide may use a suicide method that gives them time to change their mind, to call for help, or to be rescued.

- In a *completed suicide,* the person dies. Some people refer to this as a "successful suicide." They will say something like "The person succeeded in killing herself." Because we don't believe that any suicide is a success, we use the phrase "completed suicide" instead.

- A person shows *suicidal behavior* when he or she talks about suicide or gives other warning signs that he or she is thinking about or planning a suicide or is fascinated by death. Suicidal behavior does not involve an attempt to take one's life.

- Someone in a *suicidal crisis* is dangerous enough to himself or herself to attempt or complete suicide.

··

*Better yet, photocopy page 8 before filling in the blanks, especially if this isn't your personal copy of *The Power to Prevent Suicide.*

••

ANSWERS TO FIVE IMPORTANT QUESTIONS

1.   What if I try to help someone I think may be suicidal, and it turns out there's no real problem?

First, congratulate yourself for reaching out to someone you thought was in trouble. Sure, you might worry that others will think you overreacted. You might even feel a little foolish. But saving a life is a serious matter. It's much better to make a mistake and offer help when it isn't needed than to realize later that there was a serious problem and you didn't do anything to help.

2.   What if my friend just seems to be trying to get attention by talking about suicide?

It's easy to get impatient with a friend who tries to get attention by saying or doing something that seems overly dramatic. Your friend, however, must be feeling pretty awful or lonely to use suicide talk as a way to get attention. See pages 27–28 in Chapter 2.

3.   What if I think a friend may be in trouble, but no one will listen to me?

Keep telling people until you find someone who will help. Don't give up.

4.   What if someone I try to help commits suicide anyway?

Another person's suicide is never your fault. See pages 89–94 in Chapter 8.

5.   What if I think about suicide, but I don't have anyone to talk to?

Call your local crisis center or suicide hotline. On pages 117–118, you'll find information about how to find a crisis center or hotline, plus descriptions and phone numbers for three national hotlines you can call for help or information.

••

We Want to Hear from You

Please let us know what you think of *The Power to Prevent Suicide*. Tell us what helps you. If there's anything you feel that we should have included but didn't, let us know. We want to hear your thoughts, your concerns—and your success stories. You may write to us at the following address:

Dr. Richard E. Nelson and Judith C. Galas
c/o Free Spirit Publishing
400 First Avenue North, Suite 616
Minneapolis, MN 55401-1730.

We hope that after reading this book, you'll see that there are things you can do to save someone's life. We hope that you'll come to believe in your own power to make a difference in the fight against teen suicide. Young people shouldn't have to kill themselves to solve their problems. With your help, someone may choose to live.

Dr. Richard E. Nelson
Judith C. Galas
May 1994

SOURCES FOR THE FACTS AND FINDINGS
IN THIS INTRODUCTION

1. Bender, David L. and Leone, Bruno, series editors, *Suicide: Opposing Viewpoints*. San Diego: Greenhaven Press, 1992.

2. Patros, P.G. and Shamoo, T.K., *Depression and Suicide in Children and Adolescents: Prevention, Intervention and Postvention*. Needham Heights, MA: Allyn and Bacon, Inc., 1989.

3. Davis, F., "Suicidal Crises in School," *School Psychology Review* 14 (1985), 313-324.

4. Grollman, E.A., *Suicide: Prevention, Intervention and Postvention*. Boston: Beacon Press, 1988.

• •

IMPORTANT INFORMATION

The adult I trust the most to listen to me and to help me when I'm in trouble is:

_____

Work phone: _____

Home phone: _____

Address:

_____

_____

_____

A second adult I trust to listen is:

_____

Work phone: _____

Home phone: _____

Address:

_____

_____

_____

The phone number of my local crisis center is:

_____

    To find the phone number of the crisis center nearest you, look in the yellow or white pages of your phone book under "Suicide," "Suicide Prevention," or "Suicide Hotline." If your phone book does not list any numbers under these headings, press or dial "0" for operator and ask the operator to give you the number.

• •

PART ONE

....

WHY, WHAT, AND WHO

We know the topic of suicide can be scary. It might feel even scarier if you know someone who has attempted or committed suicide or if you've thought about suicide yourself.

We also know that suicide may be a subject you haven't had much chance to talk about with parents, teachers, or friends. The first three chapters of The Power to Prevent Suicide *give you the information you need to make suicide feel less scary and more like a problem you can understand.*

CHAPTER
· 1 ·

WHY WOULD SOMEONE WANT TO DIE?

Maybe you know someone who has attempted suicide. Maybe you knew someone who committed suicide. If so, then you've probably heard yourself or others ask, "Why would she want to die?" or "Why would he do something like that to his family?"

Those are natural questions, but most often they don't lead you to one right answer about why someone you know chose suicide. Here's a better question to ask: "What problem or problems was that person trying to solve?" It may sound strange to you, but most suicidal teens aren't really trying to die. They're simply trying to solve one or many problems. The tragedy is that they choose a *permanent* solution to their *temporary* problems. The most important thing to remember is that most young people who attempt or complete suicide don't want to die. What they want is to escape the problems they think are too big or too awful for them to solve. Their problems give them emotional and physical pain, and suicide seems like a sure way to make that pain stop.

How can we know for certain that the thousands of young people who committed suicide last year really didn't want to die? And if they didn't want to die, why did they die?

People who work with suicidal teens believe that most don't want to die because of the ways they try to die. Most young people attempt suicide in their own homes between the hours of 4 p.m. and midnight.[1] In other words, they attempt suicide in the one place where they are most likely to be found, and they do it during the time of day when someone from their family most likely will be around. The chance of rescue is high, and people who hope for rescue really don't want to kill themselves.

But what about the young people who weren't rescued? How can we be sure that they didn't really want to die? We can't be sure, but we can get clues about what they were thinking by talking to young people who survived suicide attempts that really should have killed them.

Each of these teens picked a time, a place, and a method of death that left little room for rescue. Some of them survived bullet wounds to the head, jumps from high bridges, or high-speed crashes into brick walls and trees. When they were asked, "What did you think as you pulled the trigger?," "What flashed in your brain when you jumped off the bridge?," "What was in your mind when you knew you were going to crash?," they consistently answered, "I wanted to change my mind."

Faced with the certainty of their own death, most said they suddenly realized their problems weren't so big that somehow they couldn't be solved. Their problems weren't so bad that somehow they couldn't find a way to survive them. In that second before they almost died, they knew they wanted to live.

But what about the more than 5,000 young people in the United States alone who did commit suicide last year?[2] Why did they die if they didn't really want to? Some died because they misjudged who would be around to rescue them during their suicide attempt. Some died thinking, "I want to change my mind." Some died because they didn't have a friend who reached out to them and got them the help they needed.

To help keep a friend from committing suicide, you need to know a little about human behavior. Knowing a little about psychology will help you understand why someone you know might choose suicide.

Most people require two basic things to feel positive about their lives:

1. *They need love.*

2. *They need to feel good about themselves.*

Most behaviors are influenced by two basic principles:

1. *People behave according to how they feel about themselves.*

2. *Every behavior has a purpose; people's actions don't "just happen."*

Once you're familiar with these key ideas and how they work in everyday life, you'll understand a little better why some young people might want to commit suicide. You'll see how a concerned and caring friend can play a significant role in reversing someone's suicidal thoughts and stopping his or her suicidal plans.

A Need for Love

All of us must feel loved before we can feel good about ourselves and our lives. This one strong need has three important parts:

1. *a need to be loved,*

2. *a need to love, and*

3. *a need to belong.*

If these three ingredients are present in our lives most of the time, we are able to cope with life's ups and downs and work out our problems fairly well.

Take school, for example. If you're an average student who has lots of friends and who gets along with most of your teachers, then you're probably not going to fall apart if you fail a history test. You may feel bad about doing poorly, and you might be embarrassed to face your teacher when she hands back the papers. You might pick at yourself for not studying the night before, and you may resolve to do better the next time. That "F" probably ruined your morning, but it didn't ruin your life. You'll still joke around with your friends at lunch, and you'll still make plans for the weekend with your girlfriend or boyfriend. You know life has a way of balancing out, and your history grade may be a pain, but it's not a disaster.

Some of the reasons you can ride out that history grade are knowing your friends and most of your teachers like you and knowing you like them. You also know you belong—you have a place among your friends and your school where you fit in. For many reasons, some young people feel disliked or unloved. They may feel like outsiders at school and even at home.

Teens who feel unloved, who don't feel love for others, and who don't feel like they belong within their families, their schools, or their neighborhoods, don't ride out their problems so easily. School failures, problems at home, and arguments with friends add to their feelings of self-hatred, worthlessness, and loneliness. When these feelings build, problems seem bigger and more difficult to solve. Even the problems these teens once might have thought were small suddenly grow in importance because their attitudes about themselves have gone sour.

Some young people have compared this lonesome, troubled time to feeling like they were drowning or being squeezed by a heavy sadness. What do you think they most needed to get them through this sad time? If you answered "a friend," you're right.

Think about it. If you're planning to commit suicide because you believe no one loves you, then having someone care enough to talk to you might give you a glimmer of hope. If you're thinking about dying because you don't love anyone, then having someone be kind to you lights a flicker of warmth in your own heart. If you want to end your life because you feel you don't fit in, then one friend can make you believe that at least you have a place with that person.

One interested, caring friend can keep someone from committing suicide because that friend helps satisfy some part of everyone's basic need for love. Sometimes all it takes is one moment of caring to give another person a reason to live.

Feeling Good about Yourself

Learning about suicide doesn't involve memorizing complicated formulas. But one simple "formula" can tell us something about the things that make us feel good or bad about ourselves: **E + IO = SC and SL**.

Written out, it means that your **E**nvironment plus your **I**nteraction with **O**thers equals your **S**elf-**C**oncept and your **S**tress **L**evel. By taking the formula apart, you can learn a lot about how and why you feel happy or sad. Let's look at the left side of the formula first.

An *environment* is a place where you can be with others. You operate in many environments including your home, school, and neighborhood. When you're with your friends, you're in a peer environment. Maybe you have even more environments such as work, church, or the basketball court. In each of these places, you *interact with others*. You talk, laugh, and argue. Sometimes you're just quiet.

Now let's look at the other side of the formula. Your *self-concept* measures how you feel about yourself. Are you glad to be who you are, or are you ashamed of yourself, or do you wish you were someone else? Your *stress level* measures how upset or calm you feel inside. Your self-concept and your stress level are directly related to how your environments and your interactions with others make you feel about yourself and your life.

● ●

WHERE DOES OUR SELF-CONCEPT COME FROM?

- Our self-concept comes from within ourselves. How we feel about ourselves, how we feel about our lives, and how we feel about our friends all affect our self-concept.

- Our self-concept comes from others. How our friends, teachers, parents, or coaches treat us and what they say to us affects our self-concept.

How would these things make you feel about yourself?

- Your parents praise you.
- You fail an exam.
- Your friends stand by you.
- Your coach screams at you.
- You make the cheerleading squad.
- Someone calls you a jerk.
- You're elected to the student council.
- You embarrass a friend.

If your environments are pleasant and you get along with people, then you're going to feel positive about yourself and your stress level will be low. Life will feel great. But life doesn't always feel great. Our environments aren't always pleasant, and we don't always get along with everyone. Real life is a mixed bag of positives and negatives. That's when the formula comes in handy, because it helps us to understand how these positive and negative things affect us.

Let's imagine that the negative things that happen to you are 100-pound weights. Try wearing one of those around your neck! The positive things that happen to you are colorful balloons that each can lift 100 pounds. Let's put those weights and balloons into the formula.

Imagine that your teacher praises you in front of the whole class, you get that date you want for Friday night, your mom ups your allowance, and you score the winning point on the basketball court. That's four separate balloons. Together they lift your self-concept so high you feel like you're floating.

Now imagine that the day isn't all that perfect. You don't get a raise in your allowance, and you don't score the winning point. That's 200 pounds of heavy weights. But your teacher's praise and that Friday-night date still give you 200 pounds of upward pull, so at least you're even.

Now imagine that your teacher embarrasses you in class, your Friday-night date cancels, you don't get that raise, and you don't score that point. Do all those weights drag you down? Maybe. It depends on how much you were looking forward to that date, how positive you feel about school in general, and how many other balloons you have in your life. As long as the weights and balloons are fairly evenly balanced more often than not, life continues to feel mostly steady and pleasant.

Now imagine a totally awful day. Your date cancels, you flunk your test, you get grounded, and you miss the winning shot in the last second of the game. How do you feel? Weighted down? Of course. After all, you're a stupid, clumsy kid with mean parents and teachers and a fickle date...at least, that's how it seems to you. How long do you feel negative about yourself and life? That depends on how many bad things have happened to you recently, how you feel about yourself when one of those really bad days strikes, and how long those feelings last.

Life's weights can feel especially heavy when a young person feels trapped under his or her load. Counselors often describe these feelings as the three "I"s—life's problems are *inescapable, interminable,* and *intolerable.* When teens feel like they can't run away from or overcome their problems, when they believe their sadness will go on forever, and when they fear they will not be able to tolerate this sadness much longer, they will see suicide as a way to escape.

Troubled, weighted-down teens may also struggle with the three "H"s—feeling *helpless, hapless* (unlucky), and *hopeless.* These feelings lead them to believe they are powerless, and this belief fills them with despair.

Life delivers a mixture of balloons and weights that lift us up and weigh us down. Young people who feel suicidal have, or feel like they have, more weights than balloons in their lives. The three "I"s and the three "H"s also help them to believe their problems are unsolvable and inescapable and they can't change the bad luck in their lives. When they feel crushed under weights that seem endless is when they're likely to think about killing themselves.

A caring friend who comes along when life feels heavy is like a balloon. A friend who's willing to listen helps to lighten the load and makes problems seem solvable. So does a friend who goes with you to find someone else who can help.

Feelings Affect Behavior

People behave according to how they feel about themselves at any given time. Think about the times in your life when you thought things were going really well and your spirits were rising higher and higher. Chances are that during those times you didn't miss much school, you got your homework in on time, and you did well on your tests. If you were playing on a team, you probably felt good about your performance. More than likely you also got along well with your friends and your parents. You acted like someone who felt positive.

When life's going well, we smile more and we're more patient with others even when they say or do things we aren't crazy about. When life's going well, we have more energy. This positive energy helps us do well in school, at work, and in our interactions with others.

When life's not going well, however, we feel and act negatively. We say and do things that reflect our unhappy, frightened, or angry feelings. During those down times, we're more likely to get in trouble at home and at school. We may pick fights, and everyone and everything bothers us. Because we feel bad about ourselves, we may behave as if we hate everyone else. We may be sulky and withdrawn. If we act angry and say mean things, others quickly withdraw from us.

Think back to a time when something sad happened to you. Maybe you broke up with your girlfriend or boyfriend, maybe you lost your job, maybe you had a terrible fight with a parent. How did you feel? How did you behave? Did your behavior reflect your feelings? Maybe your actions were similar to Larry's.

Larry went steady with Sara all through high school, but during the summer after graduation, Sara didn't seem as happy to be with Larry. They were going to different colleges in the fall, and Sara said she didn't want to go steady anymore. She didn't even want to keep seeing Larry. She wanted to be free to meet and date new people.

Put yourself in Larry's shoes. How would you feel if someone you'd loved for four years suddenly didn't want to be around you? This is how Larry described his feelings: "I felt terrible. I thought it was the end of the world. I knew there would never be another woman in my life like Sara."

What Larry felt came through in how he behaved. Right after the breakup, Larry had a severe asthma attack, which was his body's response to his high stress levels. He started to drink a lot and often got drunk. He decided that he hated all women and was rude to the women in his life. He felt depressed. More and more often, he told himself that life wasn't worth living. He thought about suicide and later explained, "I thought that would end the pain."

Larry shared his suicidal thoughts with his best friend. His friend had been worried about him. He'd seen Larry drink too much, mouth off to women, and just mope around. When Larry told him he was thinking about killing himself, his friend acted immediately. "He said I had to get some help," Larry said. "He said no one, not even Sara, was worth dying for, and he went with me to talk to my coach."

For Larry, talking to his coach made a difference. His coach told him to cut out the booze, to stop moping around, and to start doing more with the guys. Larry listened because he respected his coach and trusted his opinion. His coach also didn't forget about Larry. Every week or so, he'd ask Larry how he was doing and if he was still following his advice. A few months later, Larry started to date again. Eventually he started believing that he could have a life without Sara.

All Behavior Has a Purpose

Have you ever watched a little child who starts to whine and cry because he's sleepy? That cute kid who was all smiles and fun in the morning turns into a monster at nap time. He can't say, "Mom, Dad, I'm really bushed and will feel much better after I get a little shut-eye." Instead, he acts like a terror until an adult gets the message and puts him to bed.

Teens who are thinking about suicide have a lot in common with that tired toddler. They aren't able to talk about their feelings and pain, so they let their behaviors speak for them. Consciously or unconsciously, they hope their suicide attempt attracts attention.

This need for attention is more than a way to say, "Look at me. Love me. Find me." It's a way for the young person to signal for help. Suicidal teens can't say, "I have problems I can't solve. I should be able to, but I can't. I'm acting like I want to kill myself because I want someone to save me from my suicide plan."

If all behavior has a purpose, then the purpose of a suicide attempt is to signal for help and to let others know that the young person really doesn't want to commit suicide.

Help, Not Suicide

Remember, no matter what someone says about wanting to die, he doesn't really want death. He wants help with his problems. No matter how detailed your friend's suicide plans are, she doesn't really want to die. She wants someone who can help her feel good about living. You can be that someone.

• •

PROBLEMS AND SITUATIONS THAT HAVE PUSHED TEENS TO ATTEMPT OR COMPLETE SUICIDE

These are just some of the problems and situations we know of that have pushed some young people to suicide:

- a brother's death
- a possible pregnancy
- problems with parents
- a father's death and the sale of the family farm
- hearing loss
- failing an exam
- breaking up with a girlfriend/boyfriend
- not making the cheerleading squad
- not making an athletic team
- a drug problem
- being gay, lesbian, or confused about sexual orientation

Look at this list again and ask yourself:

- Which of these problems are temporary?
- Which could be made better with time or with help?
- Which are worth committing suicide?

• •

SOURCES FOR THE FACTS AND FINDINGS IN THIS CHAPTER

1. Johnston, J., *Why Suicide?* Nashville: Thomas Nelson Books, 1987.

2. National Center for Health Statistics, *NCHS Monthly Vital Statistics Report* 41 (7, Supplement), 1990.

CHAPTER

·2·

WHAT YOU NEED TO KNOW ABOUT SUICIDE

Because suicide threatens the lives of many thousands of young people each year, all teens should know about it and do something about it. One person like you can make a difference.

Before you can help a suicidal friend, it's important to have some basic information about suicide and about suicidal people. It's especially important to know some of the misinformation about suicide that is often more widespread than the truth. You already may have heard and believed some of this misinformation. This chapter will give you the knowledge you need to better understand a friend or acquaintance who may be in danger.

FACT: Suicide Is a Leading Cause of Death among Young People Today

Suicide is the number two killer of young people between the ages of 15 and 24 in the United States and Canada.[1] Accidents—including drug overdoses, single-car accidents, self-inflected gunshot wounds, falls from bridges and buildings, and self-poisonings—are number one.[2] People who study youth suicides think that many of these accidental deaths were really suicides that looked like accidents. If they're right, then suicide is the number one killer of teenagers today.

The National Center for Health Statistics estimated that in 1992 more than 5,000 young people killed themselves, and many experts believe that estimate is low. Besides the suicides mistakenly labeled "accidental deaths," many suicides go unreported. It's painful for families to admit that their sons or daughters committed suicide.

Sometimes the police won't call a death a suicide unless the person left a note, and most people who commit suicide don't leave notes. Sometimes the police just can't be sure if a particular death was a suicide, and they hesitate to call it one unless they're certain.

Each year, an estimated 500,000 young people attempt suicide.[3] It's hard to imagine a group that large, so think about everyone in a city like New Orleans or Denver all attempting suicide in the same year.

Study after study shows that at least one-third of all the young people in the United States have seriously thought about killing themselves. The age range for suicide is dropping, with younger and younger kids thinking about, attempting, and completing suicides. In the next ten years, the suicide rate is predicted to increase the fastest among 10- to 14-year-olds.[4]

FACT: Few Suicides Happen without Some Warning

Most teenagers who attempt or commit suicide have left a trail of clues or warning signs. They have said or done things to let others know they are in trouble and are thinking about dying. Few teens keep their intent to die an absolute secret from everyone. Most at least tell a friend about their plans.

FACT: Suicide Is Preventable

Some people think that if teenagers are suicidal, there's no way you can stop them from killing themselves. Some also believe that those who don't kill themselves the first time will keep trying until they do.

The truth is that most young people are suicidal only once in their lives. Most are dangerous to themselves only for a brief period of time—24 to 72 hours. If someone stops them from carrying out their plans and shows them where to get help, it is likely that they will never make another attempt on their lives.[5]

FACT: Talking about Suicide Won't Give Teenagers Ideas

Some people believe that discussing anything dangerous will make teens want to try it. You've probably heard people say that you can't talk to young people about drugs because they'll want to use drugs, or you can't talk to them about sex because they'll want to have sex. Some parents, teachers, and counselors don't want to mention the word "suicide" because they believe that it will give young people the idea to die.

The truth is that talking about suicide doesn't make teens want to commit suicide. Instead, it gives suicidal teens a chance to let out the idea of suicide that's been eating up their hearts and brains. If someone you know is hinting about suicide, she is already thinking about it. You won't give her any ideas she hasn't had on her own. Your willingness to talk about suicide will help her get her ideas out in the open, and suicidal thoughts that are out in the open are less likely to become suicidal behaviors.

FACT: Suicide Is Not Inherited

You might get your eye color from your mom or your dimples from your dad, but you can't inherit a gene for suicide. However, you can be at greater *risk* for suicide if someone in your family has committed suicide.

To understand this, think of a family where the parents smoke cigarettes, drink alcohol to excess, or use other kinds of drugs. Children from this family are at risk for copying their parents' harmful behaviors. These children are said to have a "suggestibility factor," or the idea that if their parents or other relatives do something, it must be okay. Of course, this doesn't mean that they have to copy their parents' behavior. They can make other, healthier choices.

FACT: Most Suicidal People Are Not Mentally Ill

Because suicidal behavior isn't seen as normal or healthy, many people mistakenly believe that suicidal people must be "crazy." They lump suicidal people together with those who are mentally ill. Some even think that suicidal people are dangerous to others as well as to themselves.

Suicidal people can behave in a "crazy" or "sick" way, but their behavior doesn't spring from a diagnosed mental illness. Instead, their actions and thoughts spring from something that's gone wrong in their lives. Also, most suicidal people are not dangerous to others. They may be angry, but their anger is directed at themselves.

Most young people who attempt or commit suicide are not mentally ill, and they are not dangerous to anyone but themselves. Most of them are struggling with short-term emotional problems that make them feel suicidal for a brief period of time. Only a small number of young people have chemical or physical problems in their brains that make them act or feel strangely for long periods of time.

You may have heard of the mental illness called manic depression, which causes extreme mood swings between great happiness and deep sadness. You may have heard of schizophrenia, which causes a person to hear or see things others don't hear or see and to behave in bizarre ways. Researchers know that manic depression and schizophrenia are related to chemical and physical abnormalities in the brain.

Serotonin, a chemical in the brain, also is being studied for its possible effect on suicide. Researchers studying serotonin and suicide have found that people who have attempted and completed suicide have lower-than-normal levels of this brain chemical. These researchers believe that serotonin may act as a "brake" for violent impulses, and people without enough serotonin may harm themselves.[6]

People who suffer from manic depression, schizophrenia, or low levels of serotonin may be deeply depressed or angry most of the time—not because their lives are miserable, but because the chemicals in their brains make them feel miserable or angry.

Some people who suffer from mental illness do commit suicide. They can't bear to live with their dramatic mood swings and uncontrollable behaviors. Most of your friends and acquaintances are probably not in this group of people.

FACT: People Who Talk about Suicide Commit Suicide

Out of every ten teens who attempt or complete a suicide, seven have told someone, in some way, about their plans.[7] So most kids who talk about suicide aren't kidding around. However, their talk makes others uncomfortable. One way people deal with their discomfort is to think or say something like "He's not serious," or "She's only showing off," or "He's just saying that to get attention." For your friend's sake, play it safe. Take any talk of suicide seriously.

FACT: Suicide Is Not Just a Way to Get Attention

Often friends and parents don't respond to a young person who says, "I'm going to kill myself." They believe the teen is just asking for attention and is trying to use them or trick them into doing something he or she wants.

If someone you know is talking about suicide, it's true that he may be trying to get attention. At the same time, he may be quite serious about suicide. To be a friend in this situation, you need to put aside your own feelings about what it means to get attention. Instead, you need to pay attention to what your friend is saying, not what you think his motives might be for talking about suicide.

It might help to remember that anyone who tries to get attention by threatening to kill himself must be feeling miserable. Anyone who tries to get attention by risking his life must be feeling desperate. Even if your friend is trying to get attention, his unusual behavior shows that he is in trouble. Something has gone wrong in his life. The best plan is to listen to what he's saying and to take his threats seriously.

FACT: Suicidal Teens Believe Their Problems Are Serious

Different people perceive the same situations and problems in different ways, and they feel their effects differently as well. What may seem trivial to one person can be the end of the world to another.

Let's say that one day your friend admits that she wants to die because of something awful that has happened in her life. You want to be sympathetic, but it's hard because that "something" doesn't seem all that important to you. Maybe her boyfriend broke up with her, or she didn't get that part she wanted in the play, or her mom is dating someone your friend doesn't like. You might think, "That's too bad, but I can't imagine wanting to die because of it." What you need to remember is that you're not the one who is feeling suicidal. Your friend is.

You probably have no trouble accepting that young people and adults often see things differently. Something that seems terrible to you might seem like no big deal to your parents, and vice versa. You might be feeling low because you had a fight with your best friend. Your parents, however, might say, "What's the big deal? You have plenty of friends."

Teens and grownups aren't the only two groups that see things differently. Friends can have different opinions about what's great, what's lousy, and what's just so-so. If your friend believes that something horrible has happened in her life, accept that she believes that. To be a good friend, you need to listen to what's hurting her and let her know you want to help.

FACT: Many Things Lead Up to a Suicide

You've heard the expression "the straw that broke the camel's back." The things that lead up to a suicide are like straw piling up on the camel's back. By itself, one piece of straw is too light for the camel to even notice. Even two pieces of straw, or a dozen, don't weigh too much. But imagine that the camel is already carrying millions of pieces of straw. At some point, one more piece will be "the last straw."

Usually people don't attempt or complete suicide because one little thing has happened to them. Most often, their suicidal act comes after several bad things have happened.

One young man attempted suicide after his dog died, or so people thought at first. Many people shook their heads and wondered why this otherwise normal young man would try to kill himself over a dog. They could understand feeling bad about losing a dog, but they couldn't imagine wanting to die because of it.

The truth is that the young man didn't really try to die because of his dog. He tried to die because within a few short months leading up to his dog's death, both his father and his beloved grandmother had died. When he lost his dog, too, it was the last loss he could tolerate. It broke him and almost killed him. He's alive today because someone in his life cared enough to reach out to him and to get him the help he needed.

FACT: No Special Types of People Commit Suicide

It would be easy to keep young people from killing themselves if only certain types of teens committed suicide. Unfortunately, there aren't any identifiable types who commit or attempt suicide.

Teenagers from wealthy homes aren't any safer from feeling suicidal than those from homes at the poverty level. Young people who are popular, who do well in school, and who get along with their teachers and parents have committed suicide, not only those who do poorly in school and who don't seem to get along with anyone.

You might think a friend is safe from suicide because he seems to have everything going for him: money, a car, lots of friends, trendy clothes. But having all those things doesn't mean he can't become suicidal. Pay attention to what your friends say and do, and not so much to what they have and how you think they should feel.

FACT: People Who Attempt Suicide Are in the Most Danger When They Start to Feel Better

Many people are shocked and puzzled when someone commits suicide just when he or she seems to be getting better. Most young people are suicidal only once in their lives. But the most dangerous time for those who might make another suicide attempt is about 80 to 100 days after the first attempt.[8]

Young people get a lot of support and attention right after they try to kill themselves. Friends, parents, and teachers pay extra attention to them, and they feel as if everyone likes them.

After about three months, people's lives start returning to normal. The friends, parents, and teachers still care about the suicidal teen, but they get interested in their own lives again. The young person seems happy, so they stop worrying and paying so much attention to him or her.

But the suicidal teen returns to normal more slowly. She may still be struggling to overcome the problems or fears that pushed her to suicide in the first place. She may feel abandoned when people go back to their regular lives, and she may decide that another suicide attempt will attract everyone's attention again.

Sometimes it takes sad or troubled teens about three months after a suicide attempt to feel good enough to start looking seriously at their lives. They may find themselves facing the same problems they had before trying to kill themselves: a broken romance, failure in school, or drug or alcohol addictions. They may decide that suicide really is the only answer. The fact that they feel better for a while gives them the energy to plan their next attempt.

Friends who seem just fine immediately after their suicide attempts may be in the worst danger. Their quick return to normal may be a sign that they are actively planning their next attempt.

They feel and look happy because in their minds they're thinking, "This will all be over soon."

FACT: A Concerned, Caring Friend Can Make a Difference

A concerned, caring friend can make a critical difference in someone's life. A concerned, caring friend can be a lifesaver.

Suppose a reporter stopped you on the street and asked, "If you knew you could save your best friend's life, would you want to?" Without hesitation, you'd answer "Yes!" What friend wouldn't want to save a best friend's life?

But you might be wondering, "Even if I wanted to, could I really save someone else's life?" The answer is still "Yes!"

Sixteen-year-old Mary's friend helped to save her life. Mary seemed to have everything. All of the students and teachers at her school liked her, plus she was a cheerleader and a good student with a B+ average. But Mary's world seemed to shatter the day she thought she was pregnant. "My parents are going to kill me," Mary confided to her best friend, Susan.

Susan could see that Mary really was upset, and that she didn't sound or act like herself. Susan knew she had to be there for Mary. "How can I help you?" she asked.

"No one can help me," Mary said. Mary looked so lost and frightened that Susan felt she couldn't leave her friend alone. She knew she had to figure out a way to help Mary. She thought about all the adults Mary might trust and decided to try to get Mary to talk with their cheerleading sponsor. "Let's go see Miss Hartman," Susan suggested. Reluctantly, Mary agreed.

Miss Hartman listened to what Mary was feeling. She suggested two plans: "Let's make an appointment with your doctor, or let's go together to talk with your parents." Mary didn't want to face her parents, so she agreed to see her doctor.

This true story had a happy ending: Mary found out that she wasn't pregnant after all. She admitted later that without the care and help she received from Susan, she might have committed suicide. Susan may have saved Mary's life because she took just a little time to be there for her friend.

Imagine that one day one of your friends shares a frightening secret, like a suicide plan, with you. The fact that your friend trusts you is probably why she's sharing her secret. The fact that your friend really doesn't want to die may be why she's talking to you. The fact that your friend believes you will try to understand is why she has turned to you. You are a key person in your friend's life, and her confiding in you is a cry for help. If this ever happens to you, remember the question, "If you knew you could save your best friend's life, would you want to?" Your "Yes!" can make a difference in the life of a friend or in the life of anyone you know or care about. If you learn how to reach out, how to listen, how to ask questions, and when to get help, you can help keep a friend from committing suicide.

In Part Two of this book, we'll tell you how you can be a suicide preventer and help a friend who's in trouble. You'll also learn how to comfort yourself if someone you know commits suicide, and how to help yourself if you're feeling unhappy about your own life. Plus you'll find some ideas on how to get your school and community involved in preventing teen suicide.

SOURCES FOR THE FACTS AND FINDINGS
IN THIS CHAPTER

1. Crook, Marion, *Please, Listen to Me! Your Guide to Understanding Teenagers and Suicide*. Bellingham, WA: Self-Counsel Press, 1992.

2. U.S. Department of Health and Human Services, "Assessment and Documentation of Youth at High Risk for Suicide," January 1989.

3. Kolehamainen, J. and Handwerk, S., *Teen Suicide: A Book for Friends, Family, and Classmates*. Minneapolis: Lerner, 1986.

4. Frederick, C.J., "An Introduction and Overview of Youth Suicide," in M.L. Peck, N.L. Farberow, and R.E. Litman (eds.), *Youth Suicide*. New York: Springer, 1985.

5. Capuzzi, D. and Golden, L., *Preventing Adolescent Suicide*. Muncie, IN: Accelerated Development, Inc., 1988.

6. Holden, Constance, "A New Discipline Probes Suicide's Multiple Causes," *Science*, Vol. 256, June 26, 1992.

7. Rickgarn, R.L., *The Issue Is Suicide*. Minneapolis: University of Minnesota, 1983.

8. Peck, M.L., Farberow, N.L., and Litman, R.E., *Youth Suicide*. New York: Springer, 1985.

CHAPTER
· 3 ·

WHAT ARE THE
WARNING SIGNS OF
SUICIDE?

As you learned in Chapter 2, no special types of people commit suicide. Teens at risk come from all kinds of families—rich and poor, happy and sad, two-parent and single-parent, active and quiet. They live in all parts of the country and come from a wide variety of ethnic backgrounds, races, faiths, and cultures.

In other words, we can't tell you to look for a brown-eyed jogger who drives a great car and loves cats. But we can help you to be alert for friends who suddenly start acting differently. Most suicidal people put out warning signs to the world, and these warning signs are their cries for help.

Suicide Threats

Most suicidal teens either directly or indirectly tell others that they plan to kill themselves. A direct threat leaves nothing to the imagination: "I'm going to kill myself," "By next Monday, I'll be dead," "I'm going to blow my brains out with my dad's gun." Direct threats should be taken seriously, even if they sound overly dramatic at the time. Few people make serious statements about killing themselves just to be dramatic or funny.

Indirect threats are harder to catch. If your friend says, "The world would be better off without me," "Sometimes I just want it to be over with," or "I wish I were dead," is she suicidal or just having a bad day? Indirect threats are tricky because they slip into casual conversation and sound a lot like something you might say when you're feeling embarrassed, tired, angry, or stressed out.

Sean Kelly's family didn't clue in to his indirect threat. His mom and brothers and sisters knew that he always spent a lot of time in his basement bedroom listening to loud music. One night his stereo shook the house. His exasperated mom screamed down the stairs, "Shut that damn thing off!" Sean screamed back, "Pretty soon it will be real quiet down here!"

For the Kelly family, this was another in a long line of squabbles with Sean, and everyone went to bed thinking he was just being surly. But in the morning, when Sean's brother went to the basement to get a pair of jeans out of the dryer, he found Sean's body hanging from the ceiling joists.

Sean's family frequently remembers his last angry words: "Pretty soon it will be real quiet down here." At the time, those words didn't seem unusual or important. After his suicide, they jumped out as a warning that he planned to commit suicide. But his indirect threat wasn't obvious before he died.

Direct or indirect threats are important clues, but indirect threats in particular can be difficult to spot. Fortunately, there are several other warning signs you can look for.

• •

VERBAL WARNINGS

If someone you know makes statements like these, he or she could be thinking about suicide.

- "I've decided to kill myself."
- "I've had it; I'm through."
- "I wish I were dead."
- "I've lived long enough."
- "I hate my life."
- "I hate everyone and everything."
- "The only way out is death."
- "I just can't go on any longer."
- "You won't be seeing me around."
- "Do you believe in reincarnation? I'd like to come back someday."
- "If I don't see you again, thanks for everything."
- "I'm getting out; I'm tired of life."

• •

Sudden Changes in Behavior

When people suddenly stop acting like themselves, it's usually a sign that something has going wrong in their lives. Remember that people behave according to how they feel at any given time. Suicidal people are weighted down with sadness, worry, and often self-hate. Their behaviors and appearance will reflect their negative feelings. Pay attention if someone you know starts to act differently in one or more of these ways.

- *Food.* Teens who were good eaters may become finicky, and light- to- moderate eaters may start to chow down. Skinny teens get fat and plump ones start to look thin.

- *Sleep.* Most suicidal teens can't seem to stay awake; they practically sleep their lives away. But some turn into night owls, pacing in their rooms or staying out late for no reason.

- *School.* Many excellent-to-average students start skipping school, and their grades hit the skids. Young people who already faced bad grades and hard times often drop out of school.

- *Appearance.* Suicidal teens frequently stop caring about how they look. They stop paying attention to their hair and clothes and they may stop showering. Young people in crisis often look rumpled and dirty, and they don't seem to care or even notice.

- *Activities.* Teenagers in pain lose interest in the things they used to love. Athletes drop their teams, musicians stop playing their instruments, and regular joggers stop running. Many also drop their friends; they stop hanging out with the gang or doing the things everyone used to do together.

- *Withdrawal.* Suicidal teens often withdraw into themselves and their rooms. They tune in to their headphones and tune out of life. Sometimes they remove themselves shyly and quietly without wanting anyone to notice. Sometimes they act as if life's just a big bore, and they let it be known that everyone and everything has become a pain. If your outgoing friend suddenly starts hanging out by himself, he may be thinking about dying.

Any sudden changes in your friend's normal behavior that go on for days or weeks can be strong clues that something is wrong. The important words are "sudden" and "changes." You're not looking for behaviors that bug you personally, but behaviors that are different for your friend. You might not like it that your friend's a natural slob who can't get up before noon, but those habits don't mean your friend's suicidal. Pay close attention, however, if that sloppy sleepyhead turns into a neat freak who can't ever close his eyes.

Significant Losses

Young people whose parents or siblings die can hurt badly enough to wish they were dead. Their daily lives have changed completely, and they must adjust not only to the loss of someone they loved, but also to the hole that person has left in their lives. Some teens can't imagine living without their mom or dad, brother or sister.

Losses from death aren't the only major losses that can hurt your friend. Breaking up with a girlfriend or boyfriend, or living through parental divorce or separation, also hurts enough to make some teens want to die.

Sometimes young people don't want to go on living after an illness or an accident has left them physically disabled. Eric, a Kansas teenager with a bright future as a musician, came down with an infection that left him deaf in one ear. The family thought Eric was taking this setback fairly well. They were pleased when he enrolled in a summer music camp.

One night when his family was asleep, Eric left his home and sat down in the middle of a dark highway. By the time the truck driver saw Eric in his headlights, it was too late to stop the rig. Eric was among the few teen suicides who left notes behind. One was to his parents explaining that he couldn't face life without his hearing; the other letter was to the driver telling him that it wasn't his fault.

Remember that everyone feels loss differently. A loss you might not think of as big enough to die for may be life-altering for your friend.

Giving Away Treasured Possessions

People who plan to die frequently give away the things that matter to them the most. A suicidal friend may pass along favorite CDs and tapes, videos, posters, a stuffed animal, a special jacket or sweater, a collection of baseball cards, and even more costly items like a stereo, bike, or sports equipment.

Young people can be generous, but be suspicious if there's no special occasion for gift-giving and if the items are particularly dear to your friend. Be on the alert if the giveaway is accompanied by words like "I won't be needing this" or "I wanted you to have something to remember me by."

Tying Up Loose Ends

In the same way suicidal teens might give away prized possessions, many want to tie up life's loose ends before they die. Young people who want to "get their houses in order" might suddenly repay a loan, answer a letter that's long overdue, return something they've borrowed, or tidy up their room, closets, and dresser drawers. These actions are not suspicious in and of themselves. In fact, any one of them can be seen as normal and responsible.

Combined with other warning signs, however, this sudden desire to take care of such details could indicate that your friend doesn't plan to be around much longer. Pay close attention if this need to get one's life in order includes talk of a will, questions about funeral homes and burial ceremonies, and an interest in music, flowers, or religious rites that would be appropriate at a funeral.

Aggression, Rebellion, and Disobedience

Teens who want to kill themselves often are angry at parents, teachers, or friends who have hurt or disappointed them. Frequently they are angry at themselves, and their anger jumps out in aggressive, rebellious, or disobedient ways. Like other behavior changes, these sudden outbursts are surprising and unusual. They can also drive other people away—a dangerous thing for a teen in trouble. No one wants to be around a mouthy, spiteful, unpredictable person, so your friend's obnoxious or hostile behavior isolates her from the very people who can help her. Isolation puts suicidal people in a lonesome and perilous spot.

If you find yourself avoiding a friend because suddenly she is just hard to be around, stop and think about what's happening. Does your friend usually display temper and aggression? Is it normal for her to be rude to her parents, teachers, and friends? Does she usually act rebellious when something doesn't go her way? Can you think of a good reason why your friend might be so angry? If you answer "no" to most of these questions, then your friend may be in a suicidal crisis and crying for help.

Self-Destructive Behavior

Some suicidal teens act like they're trying to hurt themselves or worse. They drive their cars, bikes, or motorcycles recklessly. They take chances when walking on busy streets or along cliffs, bridges, and railroad tracks.

Some may start to carry a gun. They may show off by mishandling the gun or pointing it at themselves, claiming that they're just "having fun" or "being cool."

Some young people at risk of suicide stop taking care of their bodies. They may start smoking and drinking heavily; they may take other kinds of drugs; or they may use drugs and alcohol at the same time.

Some suicidal teenagers, particularly young women, may stop taking care of their bodies by starving themselves. Those who suffer from anorexia stop eating or eat barely enough to stay alive. Those who have bulimia may vomit after each meal. Many people think these young women are starving their bodies because they want the perfect figure. Many psychologists and counselors see eating disorders as cries for help rather than as extreme ways to diet.

Sally was a good student with an easy laugh and lots of friends when she entered high school. Before she turned 16, however, she was hiding vodka in her locker and gulping it between classes. Then she started skipping school and ate almost nothing. At home she screamed "I'm so fat!" at her mirror and refused to leave the house because she said she was a blimp and looked ugly in all her clothes. Week by week, her naturally small body grew bonier.

Her confused mother thought that Sally was "going through a phase." Her school counselor was worried but couldn't get Sally to come in and talk. One day, when she was home alone, Sally slashed her wrists. Her mother found her in time, but Sally attempted suicide twice more before intensive therapy revealed that she was an incest survivor. Getting drunk and starving herself were her ways of showing how much she hated the body that had been sexually abused.

If your usually cautious and responsible friend starts taking risks or harming his or her body, you may have a friend who's thinking about suicide.

Loss of Self-Esteem

On any given day, any teen can feel like the ugliest, clumsiest, dumbest geek around. But these feelings don't last forever. Something good happens or the feelings just fade away and life returns to normal. Most young people have a core of self-respect and self-confidence that helps get them through the bad times and mood swings.

Teens who have lost their self-esteem are different. They literally look as if they have lost something. They don't stand as tall as they used to. They don't look directly into people's faces. They can be heard to say things like "I can't do anything right," or "I'm so stupid," or "No one will ever go out with me." And when they say these things, they sound as if they believe them. They don't sound as if they expect to be talked out of their negative feelings.

Young people with little or no self-esteem often perceive themselves as worthless, unimportant, and unlovable. They believe that they don't fit in, they can't do anything right, and no one cares about them. They may start believing that they would be better off dead.

● ●

REMEMBER THESE WARNING SIGNS

If someone you know...

- makes suicide threats
- shows sudden changes in behavior
- has recently experienced a significant loss
- gives away treasured possessions
- ties up loose ends
- becomes aggressive, rebellious, and/or disobedient,
- takes risks or becomes self-destructive, or
- seems to have lost his or her self-esteem,

...he or she may be thinking about suicide.

In Part Two of this book, you'll learn how to reach out to a friend who shows signs of being in trouble.

One of these warning signs by itself may simply mean that the person is going through a short-term slump. But the more warning signs a person displays, the more likely it is that he or she is suicidal and needs your concern and friendship.

● ●

CHAPTER
· 4 ·

WHO'S AT RISK?

While we can't pinpoint specific types of people who are suicidal, we do know that some young people are at higher risk for suicide because of the particular situations or problems they face. Young people at higher risk for suicide are those who:

- are depressed
- have alcohol or other drug problems
- are gay or lesbian
- have attempted suicide before, or who come from homes where someone has committed suicide
- are gifted

- have learning disabilities
- are pregnant, or
- are or have been physically, emotionally, or sexually abused.

Facing one or more of these situations or problems doesn't automatically mean that someone will be at higher risk for suicide. But it does make life more stressful. A young person under pressure from even one of these situations or problems may not have the emotional, mental, or physical energy to give to any more worries that might come along. Suicide may seem to be the only escape.

Michael's stepfather kicked the 15-year-old out when he learned Michael was gay. By the time Michael ended up at Covenant House, a shelter for homeless youth, he was a prostitute and a drug addict. With the help of the shelter's staff and his own hard work, Michael became a recovering addict. He also started feeling good about who he was and about his future.

On the day he was to leave Covenant House, Michael slashed his wrists. He later told friends he was afraid he would fail in his new life and let everyone down. Michael had struggled with being gay, having an addiction, and being homeless. The fear of failing was more pressure than he could bear. His suicide attempt was a cry for help to handle this extra stress.[1]

You also should know that certain groups of young people seem to be *less* likely to commit suicide than others. For example, African-American teens have a low suicide rate, and African-American females have the lowest suicide rate of any ethnic or racial group in the United States.[2] However, this doesn't mean that African-Americans, male or female, never commit suicide. Race and gender are no guarantee that a friend is not at risk.

When you know the warning signs of suicide, and when you know which groups are more at risk than others, you can decide on a friend-by-friend basis who might need a little extra attention, care, and understanding. This knowledge also can help you determine who among your friends might need you to get help for them when they are in danger of committing suicide.

Teens Who Are Depressed

Being depressed and being suicidal are not the same. It's possible to be depressed and never even think about suicide. Depression, however, appears to be the most common emotion experienced by suicidal teens. Frequently their feelings of sadness and hopelessness appear linked to something that upset them shortly before they became depressed.

Most young people feel sad or blue from time to time. Mood swings are common in teenagers' lives and usually last only a day or two. Situational depression is tied directly to something that has happened or is happening in their lives: doing poorly in school, breaking up with a boyfriend or girlfriend, fighting with parents, losing a job. Teens who experience one or more of these situations feel depressed, and their feelings block their ability to see reasonable solutions to their problems.

Depression can set young people up for suicide attempts because teens who are depressed often believe their troubles and sadness will never end. They believe they are unlucky, their lives will never get any better, and there is nothing they can do about it. They believe the life they are living is the life they'll always have. Often these feelings of hopelessness make them turn to suicide as an escape.

Teens who are depressed have little or no energy or interest in the people or life around them. They stop talking to other people, and they stop doing the things that have made their lives interesting. They appear sad and weighted down, they sleep a great deal, and they often talk in soft, tired voices. They act as if everything is a huge effort. Usually they go off by themselves. They fall into a bleak cycle that follows a pattern of depression, isolation, sadness, and more depression. The longer this cycle goes on, the greater the risk that they will try to end their sadness and loneliness by ending their lives.

If someone you know sounds and acts depressed, he simply may need a friend to cheer him up and coax him into doing things again. He may need a little more of your attention while he gets over a broken heart or stops feeling bad about losing his job. If he starts to give off other suicidal warning signs, or if he also belongs to another high-risk group, he may need more than cheering up. He may need a friend who will help him find the counseling and support system he needs.

Teens Who Have Problems with Alcohol and Other Drugs

Alcohol and other drugs can affect troubled teens in three ways:

1. *If someone doesn't have an alcohol or drug problem but is sad enough to be thinking about suicide, these substances can cloud the person's judgment and make him or her more willing to take chances.*

2. *If someone routinely abuses alcohol or other drugs, these substances can promote depression and suicidal thoughts.*

3. *If someone's parents are alcoholics or drug addicts, the fact that the family is falling apart can cause enough pain to make the person want to commit suicide.*

About one-third of the young people who commit suicide are under the influence of a drug.[3] Most often the drug is alcohol, and most often these teens have been drinking beer because it's cheap and easy to get. You probably don't think of beer as being deadly, but if it helps a friend decide to die, beer can be as lethal as a gun.

Most young people who commit suicide while under the influence of chemicals aren't addicted to drugs or alcohol. They have just decided to get high or drunk because they're feeling bad. The drugs or alcohol affect the part of the brain that helps them think clearly.

Have you ever seen your friends get high or drunk? Think about the things they did and said. Did they behave normally? Did they sound and act like they did when they were in school or at your house for dinner or just hanging out? Most likely your drunk or stoned friends acted out of control. Suicidal teens whose brains get blasted by drugs or alcohol find it easier to make the decision to kill themselves. They already feel sad, and the drugs and alcohol make suicide seem like the only way to stop the hurt. These chemicals also make them feel braver and more willing to take chances than when they are sober.

Drugs and alcohol also play a big part in the lives of suicidal teens whose parents are substance abusers or addicts. These young people might be drug- and alcohol-free, but their lives are filled with pain because their families are falling apart.

Some suicide experts believe that most teens who have committed suicide or are likely to commit suicide are affected in some way by alcohol or other drugs. They count the ones who got drunk or stoned just before dying, the ones who were addicted, and the ones who had addicted parents. Together these groups make up 75 percent of the young people who have committed suicide.[4]

The chances are good that if you have friends who use alcohol and other drugs, but who aren't in any danger of suicide, the drugs they use can impair their judgment and make them take chances they wouldn't think of taking when they were sober or drug-free. They may drive their cars carelessly, mishandle guns, or take dangerous dares. Alcohol or other drugs might help them decide to do things that could harm them or kill them.

According to figures distributed by the Prevention Center of Boulder, Colorado, the number one cause of death for young Americans between ages 15 and 24 is motor vehicle crashes. Alcohol or drugs are found to be related to about half of these crashes.

It's no wonder that teens touched by drugs or alcohol are in one of the highest risk groups for suicide and accidents.

Teens Who Are Gay, Lesbian, or Questioning Their Sexual Orientation

Researchers who study gay youth and suicide estimate that about one-third of the young people who attempt or commit suicide are gay or lesbian.[5] Many studies have been done on homosexuality and on the numbers of people who are gay or lesbian in America. The numbers vary depending on the report, but experts believe that about 10 percent of the people who live in the United States are homosexuals.

If gay people make up only one-tenth of the population and gay teens are about one-third of the youth who attempt or commit suicide, then gay and lesbian teens make up an unusually high number of the youth suicides.

Being a teenager can throw all young people off balance. The physical changes that come with growing up can be confusing and embarrassing. Along with these physical changes come roller-coaster emotions. Teens ache to be in love and to be close to the people they love. They ache when they are rejected. One day their love makes them ecstatic, and the next day it makes them blue.

Falling in love, having sex, and being hopelessly attracted to someone can be difficult for anyone—young or old, male or female, gay or straight. For straight people, these wide-ranging feelings and behaviors are considered normal. At least, that's what society says. But for gay people, the overwhelming message is that their kind of love is sick, perverted, disgusting, sinful, and, in some places, against the law. While straight couples feel they have every right to walk around with their arms wrapped around each other, gay couples must try hard never to touch, never to reveal what they feel and who they are.

Gays or lesbians who keep their sexual orientation a secret fear losing their job or their spot on the team, the cheerleading squad, or the student council if anyone finds out they're gay. They live with the daily stress that if they are discovered, they will be rejected by family, friends, and teachers.

Some gay or lesbian teens are open about their sexual orientation. They might not feel the daily stress of keeping a secret, but they do live with the possibility that someone will reject them for being gay or that they will be verbally abused or physically harmed.

Some young people aren't sure whether they are straight, gay, or bisexual. They may have some questions about their sexual orientation. They may wonder if they're gay because they don't date, and they may worry because they don't have a steady when everyone else does.

Some young people are the butt of jokes or name-calling because they look or act differently than other teens or have different interests. Girls who are good athletes may be called "lezzies" or "dykes." Boys who enjoy activities like acting or dance lessons might be called "queers," "sissies," or "fags." These verbal taunts make teens feel self-conscious. They may worry that if they are gay, they will always feel different and their lives will always be painful. These young people might not, in fact, be gay, but they may feel the pressures that come from being perceived as different.

If you have a friend who is being singled out as different and who is being attacked for being gay, your friend will need your support—whether he or she is gay or simply worried or wondering about being gay.

The teenage years are difficult for all young people, but for gay youth the problems are compounded by isolation, rejection, fear, and often self-hatred. If you have a gay friend, then remember that just being gay in a society where homosexuality isn't accepted can add to your friend's overall stress level. This extra stress can lead to thoughts of suicide.

Teens Who Have Attempted Suicide Before, Or Who Come from Homes Where Someone Has Committed Suicide

Most young people are suicidal only once in their lives,[6] but a small number will attempt suicide again. They are most likely to make another attempt about three months after their previous one.[7] Be especially watchful and caring when a friend nears this three-month anniversary.

Teens in this high-risk group may remain at risk for about a year. During this time, they need to know they have someone or something other than suicide to turn to when their lives get bumpy.

Young people from homes where someone has committed suicide are also at risk for attempting suicide themselves. They feel emptiness, pain, sadness, anger, grief, and often guilt over their family member's suicide. These feelings can become so overwhelming that teens start to think they just can't go on. The family member who committed suicide has already given them the idea that killing yourself is one way to deal with problems. So it's not surprising that survivors may see suicide as an acceptable way to end their own pain.

If you have a friend who has lost a member of his or her family to suicide in the past year, you need to pay special attention to him or her. Watch for the warning signs and take time to be a good listener. You'll learn how in Chapter 6.

Teens Who Are Gifted

You might find it hard to believe that your smart, talented friends have a special set of problems that put them at risk for suicide. In fact, teens who are gifted often feel enormous pressure to be perfect at all times in all areas of their lives. Many of them come to believe they are loved and admired not for themselves, but simply for the honors, grades, and awards they receive and special abilities they have. One bad test grade, a missed scholarship, a second place in an athletic competition, or some other "proof" that they are less than perfect can make them feel as if they've let everyone down, including themselves. The shame and guilt of "failure" can lead them to suicide.

Young people who are gifted in some or many ways often tend to be meticulous and thorough planners. They think things through deeply and obsessively. They believe that every decision they make about their future must be the perfect decision. Once they have made a decision, they are likely to believe that it's the only right one for them. It's difficult or impossible for them to accept the idea that they have made a mistake and should try something else.

This thoughtful, narrow planning can be dangerous, especially when it involves a suicide decision. Teens who are gifted may become determined to commit suicide simply because they have decided to do it and can't see any alternative.

Teens Who Have Learning Disabilities

Young people who have a difficult time learning and who do poorly in school often suffer from low self-esteem and depression. Both of these feelings play a role in teen suicide. In fact, one study of youth suicides in Los Angeles found that half of the teens who killed themselves had learning disabilities, or LD.[8]

You may have friends who have been identified as having LD. Maybe you have been told that you have a learning disability. We prefer to see young people with LD as having a learning *difference* rather than a disability. They must use different methods of learning to complete their studies or to master new skills.

Because these young people face special and often difficult challenges in the classroom, they are under extra stress to complete their work. Mean comments from other teens or adults may eat away at their self-esteem and may help them to believe they are stupid and will never succeed at anything.

Living with LD and its problems adds to the pressure most young people feel to do well in school and be liked by their friends and teachers. This extra dose of pressure could make a young person feel sad enough to consider suicide.

Teens Who Are Pregnant

More and more young people are becoming sexually active, and most of these sexually active teens do not use birth control. So it's no surprise that more girls are becoming pregnant at increasingly younger ages. Many of them are terrified when they suspect or discover that they are pregnant.

Most fear their parents' rejection and anger. Many are embarrassed. What will they say to their teachers and friends? What will they tell their boyfriends? Will their boyfriends abandon them? What will happen to their plans for college or careers?

The decisions they must face because of their pregnancy—adoption, abortion, parenting—also are complex. A young woman might feel that she doesn't know how to make the right choice. She may fear that her parents or her boyfriend will pressure her into a choice she doesn't want to make.

Many girls see pregnancy as an unsolvable problem. They realize that the pregnancy won't just go away, and they believe their relationships with parents and boyfriends will be ruined forever. They feel as if their lives are out of control, and they may think that choosing to die is the only real choice they have.

On the night of a high school football game, Kim told her parents to go on to the game without her. She said she had an errand to run and would get to the game in plenty of time to join her cheerleading squad. Her parents grew concerned when Kim didn't run on to the field for the opening cheer. They retraced their route home and found their daughter dead from a gunshot wound. The autopsy report told them something they hadn't known—Kim was pregnant. Her parents later learned that Kim had shared her secret with two people: a teacher and her boyfriend.

If someone you know tells you that she is pregnant, offer to go with her to get advice from an adult she trusts. It is critical that she not feel abandoned at this difficult time in her life. She must believe that she has choices and that she can make the right choices about her future.

If your girlfriend tells you she is pregnant with your baby, you also face some important responsibilities. First, your girlfriend will need your support. You are the only other person responsible for her pregnancy, and she probably will want to talk to you about what she's feeling. She might need to tell you how frightened she is about the decisions she must make and about her future.

Her pregnancy probably will surprise you. Most likely you aren't prepared to be a father. You probably had not planned on ever having to talk to your parents about a teenage pregnancy. You might worry about how this pregnancy will affect your future. You may feel embarrassed, guilty, or trapped into making decisions you hadn't planned on facing. Just like your girlfriend, you need to find an adult you trust, someone who can help you work through your thoughts and feelings.

Both young women *and* young men need to know they can count on their friends during a pregnancy crisis. If you know or suspect a friend might be facing a pregnancy, let her or him know you are there to listen and to look for an adult who will help.

Teens Who Are Abused

Unless someone tells you that he or she is being physically, emotionally, or sexually abused at home or elsewhere, it may be almost impossible for you to know about the abuse. But there are some clues you can watch for if you suspect your friend is being abused.

For example, you may suspect that a friend is being physically abused if you see bruises or cuts. Your friend might not be able to offer an easy explanation. Maybe he explains them away *too* easily, or looks away when talking about them, or just says he doesn't want to talk about the injuries.

You may wonder if a friend is being emotionally abused if he or she has little or no self-esteem, or if you hear verbal abuse between your friend and his or her parents. Emotionally abused young people often seem shy or timid, as if they are afraid to draw any attention to themselves. They have been made to feel as if they can't do anything right and are too stupid to know much about anything. So they often lack confidence and hesitate to speak up for themselves.

Sexual abuse is particularly difficult to detect because it depends on deep secrecy. Sexual abuse confuses and frightens young people and often makes them feel ashamed and dirty. Many young people keep the abuse a secret because they fear no one will believe them. Some fear the abuser will hurt them or other members of their family. Some worry that if they tell about the abuse, the police or judge will break up the family.

Cathy lived in an abusive home. Her father frequently beat her brother and had sex with her from the time she was little. Cathy knew that what was happening in her family was wrong, but she worried that her family would suffer if she revealed her secret. She had heard stories about fathers going to jail and about children being sent to foster homes. She didn't want that to happen to her family. She decided that if a social worker or school counselor ever came to her home, she would lie and say nothing bad was happening.

Not every young person makes the decision Cathy did to lie about the abuse, but most do fear losing their parents and their love or destroying the only family they have. They feel trapped. They love and depend on their parents, even if the parents are the abusers, but they also want the physical and emotional pain to stop. Caught between the abuse and the abuser, these young people are at high risk for suicide because death can seem like their only escape.

If you know or suspect that a friend is being abused, urge your friend to tell his or her story to an understanding adult. Many teachers, counselors, youth group leaders, and religious leaders have been specially trained to help young people who are victims of abuse. If your friend is being abused and refuses to tell an adult, then it is up to you. You must go to an adult you trust and tell what you know about your friend.

Sharing your friend's secret will be hard. Your friend may be angry that you betrayed his or her confidence. Once the abuse has been exposed, your friend's family may be deeply affected. The police may be involved and your friend and his or her family will be asked many embarrassing questions.

If you find yourself worrying that you might cause too much harm if you reveal your friend's secret, remember that it is much more harmful for your friend to live with abuse. No one should be left in an abusive situation. Young people who are trapped in abusive homes carry the pain of being abused throughout their lives. Many of them often attempt suicide, and many of them die.

When High-Risk Becomes At-Risk

Many young people in high-risk groups can handle their special stress as long as the rest of their lives stay in balance. It's when other things become too much to handle that they may become suicidal.

For example, let's say you have a friend who is gay. Even though he's in a high-risk group for suicide, he handles the extra stress of being gay fairly well. He has a good attitude about himself and life, his parents accept him, and he has a number of friends. He knows, however, that many people hate gays and that some try to harm them. He knows that his sexual orientation could be a problem when he looks for a job or meets new people. So his life isn't stress-free, but it's okay.

But what if someone he cares about dies, his parents get divorced, or his family moves to another town in his senior year of high school? Suddenly his life is unbalanced, and he feels all kinds of extra pressure. These personal problems can sadden and stress any young person. For your friend, they can make life even harder.

Teens in high-risk groups for suicide need two things from their friends. First, they need friends who accept them regardless of whether they are depressed, pregnant, gay, gifted, LD, or drug dependent. Second, they need friends who can give them a little extra attention when life gets particularly rough. If you have friends in high-risk groups, you can help by staying in close touch with them and being aware of the events in their lives. You can be there for them when they need you most.

SOURCES FOR THE FACTS AND FINDINGS
IN THIS CHAPTER

1. McGrady, Mary Rose, *God's Lost Children: The Shocking Story of America's Homeless Kids.* New York: Covenant House, 1991.

2. National Center for Health Statistics, *NCHS Monthly Vital Statistics Report* 41 (7, Supplement) 1990.

3. Patros, P.G. and Shamoo, T.K., *Depression and Suicide in Children and Adolescents: Prevention, Intervention and Postvention.* Needham Heights, MA: Allyn and Bacon, Inc., 1989.

4. Patros and Shamoo.

5. Bender, David L. and Leone, Bruno, series editors, *Suicide: Opposing Viewpoints.* San Diego: Greenhaven Press, 1992. See "Society's Rejection of Homosexual Teens Causes Suicide" beginning on page 100. That chapter is an adaptation of an article that originally appeared in the Alcohol, Drug Abuse, and Mental Health Administration's *Report of the Secretary's Task Force on Youth Suicide, volume 3: Prevention and Intervention in Youth Suicide* by Paul Gibson (Washington, DC: U.S. Government Printing Office, 1989).

6. Miller, M., *Training Workshop Manual.* San Diego: Suicide Information Center, 1983.

7. Rosenthal, H., *Not With My Life I Don't.* Muncie, IN: Accelerated Development, Inc., 1988.

8. Berkovitz, I.H., "The Role of Schools in Child, Adolescent, and Youth Suicide Prevention," in M.L. Peck, N.L. Farberow, and R.E. Litman (eds.), *Youth Suicide.* New York: Springer, 1985.

PART TWO

··

HOW TO BE A SUICIDE PREVENTER

You now know some important information about suicide. You know why a friend might think about or try to commit suicide. You have a list of the warning signs suicidal people send out to their friends and family, and you have descriptions of groups who are considered to be at high risk for suicide.

The next five chapters of The Power to Prevent Suicide *explain how you can help in the battle against teen suicide. You'll learn what to do for a friend who tells you, in words or actions, that he or she is thinking about suicide. You'll learn how to take care of yourself so you can avoid having suicidal thoughts. Finally, you'll learn how to get your school and community involved in helping to prevent teen suicide.*

••

WHAT SUICIDAL TEENS NEED

- Someone who will talk with them openly and honestly.
- Someone who will listen.
- Someone who will get them the help they need.

Suicidal teens need a caring friend.

••

CHAPTER
· 5 ·

REACH OUT

One day someone you know will act or sound like a teen in trouble. He or she might show one or more of the warning signs for suicide, or move into a high-risk group because of something that happens in his or her life. This person might be a close friend or someone you know only slightly. What will you do?

We know that people resist getting involved in other people's problems. Rather than go up to someone who looks troubled, you might think, "He's got parents to talk to," or "She can go see the school counselor." You might decide that these adults should be the ones to find out what's wrong and do something about it.

It would be nice if most young people could or would talk to their parents or other adults they are close to. The truth is, they don't. In survey after survey, most teens—about 90 percent—said they believed that their parents didn't understand them. Most young people believe that someone their own age makes a better listener than an adult. In fact, most of the teens who attempt or complete suicide have told a friend about their plans.[1]

Sometimes teens do make better listeners than parents. They know how it feels to be a teenager. Parents might be defensive, uncomfortable, or hurt to hear that their son or daughter is having serious problems. They often don't want to hear that a child is unhappy enough to want to die. They fear that talk of suicide must mean there's something wrong with them or with the family as a whole. Rather than being willing to look at possible family problems, they deny that their child is serious about suicide. They find it difficult to reach out to learn what's wrong or try to help.

Young people like you are on the front lines of the war against teen suicide. You're in that spot because most teens trust other teens more than they trust adults. Like it or not, it may be your job to help a friend who is thinking about suicide.

So what should you do when you notice that someone you know seems troubled? The first thing you might have to do is work up your courage. It's hard to go up to a casual friend and start a personal conversation. Sometimes it's even hard to start a personal conversation with a close friend. Asking questions is a good way to reach out and start any conversation.

Ask the Right Questions

What questions should you ask someone who seems troubled? The same questions you'd ask anyone who seems changed or who looks down in the dumps: "What's the matter?" "Why so sad?" "Why are you avoiding everyone?" "Why didn't you come to the party last night?" "Are you feeling okay?" "Have you lost a lot of weight?" "Have you been getting enough sleep?" These questions show normal curiosity and interest in another person. Depending on your friend and the situation, you'll probably come up with dozens of other perfectly good questions to ask.

Your questions and interest will help your friend open up and start talking. Once this happens, however, you might hear frightening and disturbing things. For example, your friend might say, "I just don't want to live anymore." How will you respond?

Don't be surprised if you hear yourself saying or thinking something like this: "Cut it out. That scares me." It can be hard to hear someone else's troubles. Sometimes we're embarrassed; sometimes we simply feel that we aren't smart or clever enough to help. As a way to protect ourselves, we say or do something that gets the other person to stop talking.

When you reach out to people who may be thinking about suicide, your goal is to get them talking for as long as they want. No matter how uncomfortable your friend's words make you feel, what he's feeling is even more uncomfortable for him. You can help lighten his load if you encourage him to get his troubles out in the open. Your honest talk and careful listening will give your friend three critically important messages:

1. *I take you seriously.*

2. *I care about you.*

3. *I want to help.*

When a friend displays one or more of the suicide warning signs, you must also get him or her to think about and answer four direct and important questions:

1. *Are you thinking about killing yourself?*

2. *How do you plan to do it?*

3. *When do you plan to do it?*

4. *Where do you plan to do it?*

Does the bluntness of these questions shock you? Their very bluntness may be just what it takes to make it possible for your friend to share the secret that he wants to die. Your directness tells your friend that you really are trying to understand and you really do want to help.

These questions will give your friend permission to talk about his suicidal thoughts and the problems he's struggling to solve. Many people are surprised to learn that suicidal persons are amazingly honest about their plans. They are not evasive or dishonest when they are asked direct questions. Many are glad to be asked because this shows that someone is taking them seriously. They believe that the listener understands and wants to get involved.

So if you ask a suicidal friend if he plans to kill himself, the chances are excellent that he will tell you the truth. His answers will give you important information about how dangerous he is to himself. Answering your direct questions also may stop his suicidal thoughts from building to the point at which he spontaneously decides to act on his plan.

•••

GET YOUR FRIEND TALKING

- Talking gets the problem out in the open.
- Talking eases stress and tension.
- Talking gets you both thinking about where you can go for help.

•••

The Spontaneous Plan

Suicide is sometimes called a "spontaneous plan." How, you might ask, can a plan—something that is thought out in advance—also be spontaneous?

Think of a loudly ticking alarm clock you've set to go off at midnight. For hours you hear "tick, tick, tick, tick." Even as you sleep, you subconsciously hear the ticks as the clock's hands inch toward midnight....

Rinnnnnng! The alarm shatters the night's silence and you jump awake. You jump even though you planned for the alarm to ring at midnight. Your jump was a spontaneous reaction to your plan.

As a suicidal person's pain grows, as life becomes more uncomfortable and painful, he or she plans an escape. But the actual suicide attempt happens spontaneously, like your jump when the alarm rings. In other words, you can plan for something and still react spontaneously.

Most young people are suicidal only once in their lives, and they are dangerous to themselves only for about 24 to 48 hours. When you step in and ask your friend those direct questions, you decrease the chance that she will act spontaneously or react to that suicide alarm clock. Many suicidal people who are stopped from making one suicide attempt never plan another. So by reaching out to your friend, you can save a life.

Assess the Danger

What if your friend answers, "Yes, I think about killing myself"? Is she in immediate danger? That depends on what answers she gives to the other three suicide questions: How? Where? When? Before you can decide if your friend is really dangerous to herself, you need to understand how deadly or lethal her plan is.

A suicide plan is lethal (likely to bring about death) if:

- the chosen method usually is fatal,
- the method is available, and
- your friend plans to commit suicide at a time or in a place where there is little chance for rescue.

Plans that depend on using a gun, hanging, jumping from a high place, or crashing a car are considered more lethal than those that depend on slashed wrists, carbon monoxide poisoning, or a drug overdose. That's not to say that people don't actually die from slashed wrists, gas, and drug overdoses; they do. These methods are considered less lethal only because they give the person more time to change her mind and go for help. If the person is found before she dies, there's a greater chance the damage can be repaired or the danger reversed.

People can die instantly from a gunshot wound, but it may take several hours for someone to die from a drug overdose, carbon monoxide, or razor slashes. Stomachs can be pumped, oxygen can be given, and wrists can be sewn, if someone finds the person in time.

• •

**GUNS ARE THE LEADING METHOD
OF SUICIDE DEATHS**

• •

A Lethal Plan

In answer to the other three suicide questions, your friend confides that she plans to shoot herself in the head. She tells you that she knows where her father keeps his gun. She also tells you that she plans to kill herself on Friday night, after her parents leave for a party and before they return home at 10 p.m.

You now know that your friend plans to shoot herself, she has access to a gun, and she plans to pull the trigger when no one is around to talk her out of it or rush her to the hospital.

Your friend has just shared a lethal suicide plan. If this were a real-life situation, you could not leave her alone. You would immediately call an adult so that person could notify your friend's parents, stay with her, remove the gun from the house, or all three.

You would not, under any circumstance, go to your friend's house on Friday night and attempt to take the gun away from her. Your friend probably wouldn't turn on you, but you could be injured in a struggle for any weapon.

If you couldn't reach an adult, you would dial the emergency number 911 and speak directly to a police officer. The officer most likely would come to where you and your friend were. If your area does not have 911 service, dialing "0" would connect you to an operator who would send assistance.

In this imaginary situation, your friend truly would be in danger of committing suicide. She would need immediate help.

A Less Lethal Plan

Now let's imagine another situation: Your friend tells you that he plans to jump off a bridge.

Jumping off a bridge also is lethal. Few people survive such a jump, and there is nothing a bystander can do to save the person once he or she has jumped.

Your friend's plan sounds lethal, but you know there are no bridges anywhere around your town. So his chances of dying from jumping off a bridge are more remote. He would have to travel a long distance to find a bridge to carry out his plan.

Does that mean he's joking or he shouldn't be taken seriously? No. A wish to die should always be taken seriously. Your friend's plan to die by jumping off a bridge means he's suicidal, but he's not in immediate danger.

You would still tell an adult about your friend's plans so that someone could help him through the problems he thinks only death can solve. If he continued to think about suicide, he could get closer to forming a plan that actually would cause his death.

Ambivalence

You might wonder why someone would come up with a suicide plan that isn't really likely to cause his death. The truth is that most suicidal people feel like they want to die and live at the same time. This ambivalence creates confusion in their minds and makes it almost impossible for them to think clearly.

Can you remember the first time you stood on the high dive, the first time you stood backstage waiting to play the piano in front of an audience, or the first time you had to get up in front of a class and give a speech? Part of you wanted to make that dive, perform that piece, or give that talk. You wanted to hear the cheers, the applause, and the praise.

But an equally big part of you didn't want to take the risk. You were afraid and nervous. You didn't know what to expect or if you'd succeed. Most likely you did the dive, played your song, or gave your talk. True bravery probably had little to do with why you completed the task. You felt you had little choice. Your friends were standing behind you on the diving ladder laughing and daring you to jump, your parents were staring at you from the audience, or your teacher was waiting to give you an "F" if you didn't stand up and open your mouth. You probably thought, "I just have to get this over with."

Your suicidal friend is thinking about something much more serious than whether or not to jump into a swimming pool. Your friend is trying to decide whether or not to die. Although the two decisions are very different, they have something important in common: the feeling of not having a choice, and the desire to just get it over with.

Constricted Thinking

Suicidal people believe they have no choice but to commit suicide. That's what makes suicide plans so dangerous. As your friend's anxiety grows, as he feels more and more trapped by painful feelings and problems, the more he begins to see only two choices: "I must live with these terrible feelings," or "I must die to escape them." Your friend is experiencing "constricted thinking." He sees only two choices—life or death.

• •

TEENS WHO ATTEMPT SUICIDE...

- see their problems as unsolvable
- see suicide as the only answer.

• •

Imagine that you're walking down a lonely, dark sidewalk and you enter a narrow, curving tunnel that's just wide enough for one person. You must go through the tunnel to get to a park on the other end. The farther into the tunnel you go, the darker it gets, the closer the sides feel, the less air you can breathe, and the more alone and frightened you feel. Suddenly you feel trapped; you believe you will never get to the tunnel's other side. All you can see is darkness behind you and in front of you. You are convinced that you will suffocate. You freeze. Rather than continuing to walk forward, you stop in your tracks.

Now imagine that a friend is standing at the other end of the tunnel, the side that starts in the park. She's worried about you because you're taking such a long time. She decides she must go in and get you out. When she finds you in the tunnel, she grabs your hand and starts pulling you forward.

Because the tunnel's curves block the light ahead, the tunnel seems black and endless, and you're afraid to keep following your friend into the darkness. Part of you resists her pulling, but part of you is glad to be holding tight to her hand. Part of you wants to believe she will rescue you into the sunlight.

Pop! She pulls you into the park and into warm, bright daylight again. When you look back over your shoulder, you see that the creepy tunnel you thought was endless really was less than a block long. You take a deep breath and let it go with a huge sigh of relief. You look at your friend's smiling face and you feel safe. Together you head off into the park.

Suicidal people don't believe they can make it through the tunnel. Life has become too depressing and too intolerable. Talking things through with a counselor, facing their parents, revealing secrets about sexual abuse, coming to terms with their homosexuality, learning how to live without someone they love—none of these things seem possible.

Suicidal people live in the present: "I am trapped *now*. I am afraid *now*. I hurt *now*." Their constricted imaginations cannot take them into tomorrow or next week, much less next month or next year.

Time makes painful things less painful. With time, problems can be solved. But suicidal people can't think about time. They can't imagine there's a park just a few feet outside the tunnel. They need a friend to reach out and pull them into the sunlight.

● ●

THINGS TO THINK ABOUT AND DO

1. How do you react when someone tells you something personal? Are you embarrassed? Curious? Do you want to hear more?

2. When was the last time you told a friend something that was hard to share? Why was it hard to tell your friend? What did your friend do or say that made it harder or easier for you to share what was on your mind?

3. Try to remember the last time you felt like you wanted to escape something unpleasant. What did you want to escape? Why? What helped you get through the unpleasantness?

4. It's often easier to tackle something difficult or strange if you practice it a few times. Have a friend imagine that she's planning to run away from home and how she plans to do it. Then practice asking these four questions:

• Are you thinking about running away?

• How do you plan to do it?

• When do you plan to do it?

• Where do you plan to go?

Assess how likely it seems that your friend really will run away. Then evaluate the dangers in her plan.

SOURCE FOR THE FACTS AND FINDINGS
IN THIS CHAPTER

1. Allen, Nancy H. and Peck, Michael L., "Suicide and Young People," brochure prepared by the American Association of Suicidology in cooperation with Merck Sharp & Dohme, West Point, PA, 1975.

CHAPTER
· 6 ·

LISTEN

Helping begins when someone listens, so being a good listener is an important part of helping a friend through a suicidal crisis. When you're a good listener, you:

- help your friend get his or her suicidal thoughts out in the open,
- let your friend know you care, and
- help your friend feel that he or she is not alone.

Being a good listener does not mean that you:

- must solve your friend's problems,

- are responsible for saying the one right thing, or
- must make everything okay in your friend's life.

We know it's hard to be a good listener, but we have confidence in your ability to try and learn how to listen well. We know you've had lots of experience with people who have listened to you. You've also had experience with those who only pretended to listen, and with those who didn't listen at all. Thinking back to those experiences will help you improve your own listening skills.

We also believe that this hard job of listening is based on common sense, practice, and just being yourself. We know you don't need to be an adult or to have a college degree to work with basic listening ideas and skills. All you need is the willingness to try.

Be an Active Listener

The key to being a good listener is knowing how to be an *active* listener. An active listener does more than just *hear* someone talk. An active listener *pays attention* to what's being said.

When you *hear* music, for example, the sound just travels into your ears. But when you *pay attention* to the music, the lyrics, melody, and beat really connect with you. The sound not only travels into your ears, it also makes you feel something. It touches your mind and your heart.

When you're an active listener, you let your friend's words become like the lyrics that touch your mind and heart. You "get into" your friend's words, emotions, and behaviors, just like the times when you "get into" a song.

There are two skills that will help you to be an active listener:

- having empathy, and
- being a word detective.

Developing these skills will make you the kind of listener a friend in trouble needs.

Have Empathy

When you listen to a friend who's hurting inside, try to imagine what he or she must be feeling. When you try to feel what someone else is feeling, you're showing empathy. Empathy is the ability to experience someone else's feelings as if they were your own. It's as if you're crawling into the other person's skin, trying to understand how he or she might think and feel.

Imagine that you have a friend named Tom who's brokenhearted because his grandmother just died. You can see that Tom is sad, but you really can't put yourself in his shoes. Both of your grandmothers died when you were a baby, so you've never had a special connection to a grandmother. But Tom did. When you listen to him talk about his grandmother, you can start to understand his feelings for her: "I'm going to miss her so much. She always made me laugh, even when no one else could. To her, I was always someone special."

If you dig deep into yourself, you can remember what it felt like to miss someone. You know how much fun it is to have special times with someone and to have someone treat you as if you're special. You can imagine how it would feel to lose those special times and love. So even if you didn't have the same experience as Tom, you can imagine how it might feel to lose someone you care about very much. You can imagine how miserable you would be. You can feel empathy for Tom because you can crawl into his skin and feel his sadness.

Young people who are talking about killing themselves need an empathetic listener. They need someone who will try to imagine what they are feeling. If they hear "I understand," or "I've felt like that," or "You must feel frightened," they won't feel so alone with their feelings. They will think, "My friend really is trying to understand me."

Be a Word Detective

An active listener is a detective hunting for clues that reveal how a friend feels. As a word detective, you'll listen to:

- what your friend is saying,
- what your friend isn't saying, and
- what the words (spoken and unspoken) tell you about your friend's feelings.

What's Being Said?

A good listener listens to what's being said. But sometimes this isn't as easy as it sounds.

Have you ever only partly listened to a friend? Instead of paying attention to every word he was saying, you were busy thinking about what you would say next. Maybe your friend started to ask a question and you blurted the answer before he got the whole question out. Or maybe your friend was trying to talk about a problem, but you were already thinking about the advice you would give her.

When you're a word detective, you give all of your attention to what your friend is saying. You don't think about what you're going to say next, or where you're going with your friends on Saturday, or how much homework you have to do tonight, or why your little brother is such a pain. You focus on your friend.

What's Not Being Said?

Have you ever thought that a friend was holding something back? Maybe she talked a lot but looked sad, and nothing she said gave any hint of why she was unhappy. Sometimes people who are upset or troubled will talk about everything except how they feel.

Imagine that you have a friend named Stephanie who announces that she and her boyfriend have just broken up. "He's a jerk," she says. "I was going to break it off anyway. He saved me the trouble." She tells you every detail of their last fight. She even tells you what she was wearing, but not once does she tell you how she feels.

You know that Stephanie was really in love with her boyfriend. She talked about him all the time, and they did everything together. You also know how painful it is to break up with someone. So even if Stephanie can't bring herself to say that she feels hurt and abandoned, you can figure out that's how she feels. By reading between the lines, you know that she probably could use a friend.

What Do the Words Tell You about Your Friend's Feelings?

Figuring out what a friend's words tell you about his or her feelings is probably the most important skill a good listener can have.

It's also the most difficult to learn. As you listen to Stephanie tell you about the break-up with her boyfriend, you have to listen for the feelings behind the words she is sharing. You have to "translate" her words into the feelings.

She says: "So what if no one cares about me."
Translation: "I feel unloved."

She says: "I'm dropping out of this stupid school."
Translation: "I feel like I don't belong here."

She says: "I have nothing to live for."
Translation: "Maybe things would be better if I killed myself."

A word detective wants to "break the code" to what a troubled friend is thinking and feeling.

● ●

PHYSICAL CLUES TO WATCH FOR

Suicidal teens sometimes give physical clues that they're in immediate danger. *Get help quickly* if your friend:

- sounds upset or angry
- looks agitated
- has difficulty sitting still, or
- can't concentrate on what you're saying.

We know that most people sound upset or angry once in a while. They also can look agitated and find it hard to sit still or concentrate. These behaviors alone don't mean that they are suicidal. But these behaviors should make you suspicious if they:

- start for no apparent reason,
- sound or look really intense,
- last for days, sometimes weeks, or
- come at a time when you know or have reason to believe that your friend is under a great deal of stress.

● ●

Active Listening Do's and Don'ts

As an active listener, you want to give your friend three important messages :

1. *I'm interested in you.*
2. *I care about you.*
3. *I want to help.*

To communicate these messages, follow these simple tips:

- DO find a quiet, private place to talk. You and your friend will both be more relaxed and comfortable.
- DO sit down next to your friend.
- DO lean toward your friend.
- DO turn your face toward your friend's face.
- DO make frequent eye contact.

To make sure your message gets through, follow these suggestions:

- DON'T criticize or judge your friend. Try not to say things like "You're always in some kind of crisis."
- DON'T evaluate your friend's feelings and thoughts. Try not to say things like "That doesn't sound so awful to me."
- DON'T give advice too quickly. Try not to jump in with "Here's what I think you should do...."
- DON'T fall back on clichés. It's natural to want to come up with quick answers to complex problems, but a good listener works hard to avoid the standard lines many people use to convince others that their troubles really aren't that bad. Try not to say things like "Everything will look brighter in the morning," "Sleep on it; you'll feel better," "If you think *you* have problems...," and "Every cloud has a silver lining."
- DON'T try to jolt your friend out of his suicide plan by asking him to imagine how bad his parents will feel if he dies, or how much his girlfriend will cry. Suicidal people truly can't think about how anyone else feels or might feel. All they know is how *they* feel. Asking your friend to think about someone else's feelings sends the message, "I'm worried more about how your suicide will affect others. I'm not as worried about you."

Be Positive

Your troubled friend needs you to be a good listener. He needs you to have empathy and to be a word detective. The last thing he needs is for you to be as negative as he is. How could it possibly help him if you say, "You're right; school stinks; life stinks; everything stinks—why should anyone go on living?"

You need to be positive, but without making your friend's problems sound trivial, silly, or wrong. One way to be positive is to remind your friend of the good qualities he has or how much you care about him.

> *He says:* "I'm such a jerk. I never do anything right."
> *You say:* "Don't forget what a good drummer you are."

> *He says:* "No one's interested in what I think."
> *You say:* "I'm interested. You have good ideas."

> *He says*: "I'm stupid."
> *You say:* "You got a B on your theme paper last week."

Don't be surprised if your friend rejects or can't hear any of your positive comments. Remember the formula from Chapter 1, E + IO = SC and SL (Environment plus Interaction with Others equals Self-Concept and Stress Level)? That formula teaches that the negative things that happen in young people's environments and interactions affect their self-concept. The more negatives they experience, the worse they feel about themselves.

Like all equations, this one can be turned around. A poor self-concept combined with a lot of stress can make someone feel negative about his environment and his interactions with others. He may feel negative even when something positive happens, simply because everything is colored by his low self-image and high stress.

How can you make your friend hear and believe the positive things you're saying about him? First, keep saying positive things. Repeat them until you think your friend not only *hears* but also *listens* to what you are saying. You can also ask your friend to repeat something positive you've just said.

> *He says:* "I'm no fun anymore."
> *You say:* "You've made me laugh many times."

> *He says:* "No one likes to be around a grump."
> *You say:* "We've had some fun times together."

Your friend sighs and stares at you.

You say: "Repeat what I just said."
He says: "You said we've had some fun times together."

At this point, your friend might think back on one of those times, and he might let go of a small chuckle. That chuckle doesn't mean that everything's better. It means that for a moment your friend *listened* to what you were saying. It means that you helped him remember something positive. That brief moment may make it possible for him to hear something else that's positive. Inch by inch, positive words and feelings may help your friend move farther away from his plan to commit suicide.

What If You're Afraid You're Not a Good Listener?

One reason it's hard to listen to people talk about their troubles is that often we don't know what to say. When we see someone hurting, we want to open our mouths and say exactly the right thing. We want to sound wise and caring. We want to say something funny to lighten the moment and something helpful to make the other person feel better.

If you don't know what to say to a hurting friend, here are some simple things you could say:

- "I can see you're upset."
- "You sound unhappy."
- "I'm sorry you feel so bad."
- "How can I help?"
- "Where can we go together to talk to someone?"
- "What should we do next?"

Notice that none of these sentences are clever, wise, or witty. You don't have to be a great speaker to say any of them. The first three simply respond to what you're seeing or hearing. The last three tell your friend that you're willing to do something to be helpful or to get help.

So don't let the fear of saying the wrong words or of not saying the perfect words keep you from encouraging your friend to talk. It's not what you say or don't say that's important, but how you say it. If you sound concerned, caring, friendly, and interested, your friend will respond to those feelings.

You don't have to be a good talker to be a good listener. You don't have to be a brilliant problem solver to be a good listener. In fact, you shouldn't think that by agreeing to listen you are agreeing to be a superhero and make everything right in your friend's life. You aren't promising to solve all of his or her problems now or later. The only promises you can make to your friend—and yourself—are to be a friend who will listen, and to find an adult who can help.

If You're Still Unsure about Your Skills...

Don't underestimate your abilities to help a friend, even to save a life. If your friend has opened up to you, that's the best clue that she believes you can help. If your friend chooses to share his thoughts about suicide with you, he's letting you know he trusts you. By sitting with you and talking, your troubled friend is clearly communicating a message he or she can't put into words: "I really don't want to kill myself. I'm counting on you to help me get help. Please, grab my hand and pull me out of my dark tunnel."

Be Yourself

Are you wondering how you should act when you're with your friend and trying to help? It's simple: Do what feels comfortable to you. Are you a hugger? Then put your arms around your friend and squeeze. Are you the quiet type? Then sit close to your friend and let him or her do the talking. Are you an upbeat, talkative person? Then don't be afraid to talk in hopeful, positive, and encouraging words. Just be yourself.

● ●

THINGS TO THINK ABOUT AND DO

1. Think back to a time when you knew that someone wasn't listening to you. What did that person say or do that let you know he or she wasn't listening? Now think about a time when you felt as if you had someone's undivided attention. What did that person do or say to give you that message?

2. Find a friend to have a conversation with. Decide who will talk and who will listen. The talker must talk about anything for two minutes, and the listener must act like he or she is not listening. Afterward, talk about how the listener acted. Talk about how the talker felt.

3. Switch roles and have another conversation. This time, the listener must act as if he or she is listening to every word. Afterward, talk about how this conversation was different from the first one. How did the listener act? How did the talker feel?

4. Make a list of the things you can say and do to let a person know you are listening to what he or she is saying.

● ●

CHAPTER

7

GET HELP

One day your friend (let's call her Jennifer) confides, "I'd be better off dead. I'm going to kill myself." She tells you that she plans to take her parents' car and crash into the highway overpass a mile from her house. She trusts you to understand, and she asks you not to tell another soul. She even makes you promise to keep her secret.

From what you've learned about suicide, you know that you should take Jennifer seriously. Her suicide talk and her demand that you keep her secret have given you two things to worry about: keeping her safe, and keeping her friendship. You may feel caught between wanting to help and not wanting to break your promise.

One thing's certain: *No one should keep a suicide wish a secret,* not even if it means risking a friendship. No matter how skilled you are at listening, you can't take care of your friend all by yourself. No matter how persuasive you are at getting Jennifer to talk about her problems, you can't carry the burden of her safety alone. You can't protect her from herself every minute of the day. Her father or mother, a school counselor, a teacher, a priest, minister, or rabbi—or any adult who cares about her—must be told, and you are the one who must tell. Then the adult will intervene to get Jennifer the help she needs to work through her suicidal crisis.

Will Jennifer be angry with you for telling someone else? Maybe...and maybe not. More than likely, she told you her secret because she wants someone to help her. She also might be relieved to know that others will rush in to protect her and stop her from completing her plan.

But there's a chance she won't be relieved. She simply may be angry with you. Later she may refuse to see you or speak to you, and her anger will hurt you. It may even make you wonder if you did the right thing by telling an adult about her suicide wish.

Telling someone is *always* the right thing to do. Even if revealing your friend's secret makes her angry, it's still the right thing to do. It's much better to have a friend be angry with you for a few days, weeks, or months than to lose a friend to suicide forever.

Think of it this way: If your friend fell down the stairs and landed at the bottom with a broken leg, you wouldn't just stand around and wonder if you should go for help. You'd go—fast. You wouldn't let your friend talk you out of going because she said she was too embarrassed to let anyone know how clumsy she'd been, too afraid to go to the hospital, or too timid to trouble her parents. You'd know that your friend needed professional help immediately.

Someone who wants to commit suicide is hurting every bit as much as someone who breaks a leg, but the pain is inside, where no one can see it. The emotional pain that pushes a person to want to die won't go away by itself any more than a broken leg will heal itself properly without being cared for by experts.

Who Should You Tell?

In the fall of 1990, a 17-year-old Minneapolis girl committed suicide. Her father later told a newspaper reporter that his daughter had seemed fine until about a month before she died. The family had gone to their lake cabin for a vacation. Instead of spending her days water skiing, like she usually did when she was at the lake, the girl spent a lot of time sleeping. Her dad remembers that she mentioned a couple of times that she was having "difficulty with people."

After she died, the family learned that she had written a letter to a friend describing her despair and weariness with life. The friend didn't mention the letter to anyone. If the friend had known something about the warning signs of suicide, she probably would have told someone about the letter right after she received it.

What if one of your friends shares a secret about being tired of life or wanting to die? Who should you tell? The answer to that depends on how well you know your friend's parents, where you live and go to school, and who you trust.

If you know your friend's parents and feel comfortable talking with them, then tell them what you know. But don't tell only them. It's not unusual for suicidal teens to feel alienated from their parents. When speaking with 30 young people ages 13 to 24 who had attempted suicide, an interviewer heard them all say that they never would have tried suicide if they felt their parents supported them.[1] So even if you like and trust your friend's parents, remember that your friend may not feel the same way about them. In fact, your friend's wish to die may be triggered by problems at home—problems you have never witnessed and know nothing about.

- Some parents seem to fight with their children more than they listen to them. They may see your friend's thoughts of suicide as one more thing to fight about. They may even assume their child is just trying to get attention by pretending to be suicidal.

- Some parents are physical, emotional, or sexual abusers who would not want any outside helpers talking with their child.

- One or both parents may suffer from alcoholism or drug addiction and may not be able to be honest enough about the family's problems to get help for your friend.

It may be hard to think about, but your friend's parents may be one reason—maybe even the main reason—why he or she is thinking about suicide.

Even in loving homes, some parents find it hard to believe that their child really wants to die. They may deny any problems and take a wait-and-see approach. If they wait in the hope that your friend's crisis isn't that serious or is likely to pass, they run the risk of waiting too long.

To be sure that your friend gets the best possible protection and help, tell someone else in addition to his or her parents. That someone can be any adult(s) you trust: your own parents, a relative, a favorite teacher. Don't stop telling adults about your friend until *at least* one person tells you that he or she will do something to get help.

You don't have to tell your friend's parents if you don't want to. Maybe you don't know them, or you don't feel comfortable talking to them about their son or daughter. But you must tell someone else. The adult you confide in, or the people that adult turns to for help, will make sure the parents learn their child is in danger.

You may attend a school where people are trained in teen suicide prevention. These people might be guidance counselors, the school nurse, social workers, coaches, or perhaps the principal. They should know how to intervene to protect your friend. They will probably ask you specific questions: "What did your friend tell you?" "How does she plan to kill herself?" "Where?" "When?" Be completely honest with them, and tell them everything you know. Your information will help them decide how quickly they must act.

If you talk to someone at your school, and that person doesn't respond in a way that feels right to you, find someone else to talk to. Keep looking until you feel confident that you've found someone who can help your friend.

You may live in a community that has an emergency telephone hotline. The people who answer these phones are trained in crisis intervention. They'll ask you over the phone for all the information they need to put helping people in touch with your friend and his or her family. For help finding a hotline, see pages 117–118.

Go Together for Help

Sometimes a friend will confide that he wants to die, but he hasn't yet formed a plan. So he's not in immediate danger, but he's still in trouble. Because he's shared his feelings, you can be pretty sure he's talking to you as a way to reach out for help. But he must also share his feelings with an understanding adult before he can begin to heal his life.

You can help him take that necessary first step by suggesting he talk to an adult he trusts and by offering to go with him. You've probably heard the expression "I'll be there for you." Friends often say it to one another. The words mean "I'll stand by you during the hard times." If your friend is suicidal, you may need to go with him when he talks to his parents, counselor, or other trusted adult. You may need to stand by him.

Young people who are thinking about killing themselves feel alone in the world. Because of their suicidal thoughts, they find it hard to believe that anyone understands or cares about them. So it makes sense that when they go to an adult to talk about their problems, they may need to go with a friend who has shown concern and understanding.

Don't be hurt or angry, however, if your friend refuses your offer to go with him. He might not be comfortable having another person present during that hard conversation with parents or a counselor. Your friend may prefer privacy.

Make Sure an Adult Knows

But just because your friend says, "I'll talk to my parents, but I'd rather do it alone," doesn't mean that he will really do it. People think about dying because they're hurting, and people who hurt inside can't always make clear-headed decisions about their own safety. So, with or without your friend at your side, you must be sure to tell an adult that your friend is suicidal and possibly in danger. Keep telling adults until at least one tells you that he or she will do something to make sure your friend gets help.

What Next?

Your friend will still need you even after she has started getting help. Once her suicide plans are out in the open, she and her family will have to work hard to understand what's gone wrong in her life. It's not easy to work through the kinds of problems that lead to feeling suicidal, so the next few months or year will be painful for her.

She also may be embarrassed about that suicidal time in her life. She may be self-conscious and worry that people will think she's crazy. After the crisis has passed, she may even feel awkward talking to you and may keep her distance from you. But more than ever, your friend will need to know that you haven't abandoned her.

If she doesn't resist being with you, keep talking and doing things together. If she does resist at first, keep in touch in small ways. A quick "How are you?" phone call, short notes taped to her locker, a funny card, or small gifts like a bouquet of flowers, a book, or a tape you think she'll enjoy will let her know you haven't forgotten her. In whatever ways you can, keep being a friend.

Peer Helpers

Some schools and communities have created peer helping programs where trained students and adults work together to fight youth suicide. These teen-on-teen assistance programs train young people to give their peers problem-solving skills, information on the kind of problems many young people struggle with, and help in finding professional resources.

One peer helping group, Natural Helpers, was started in 1979 following the suicide of a high school student in Mercer Island, Washington. The counselors wanted students to help them find other students who were in danger of attempting suicide. Today this program operates in hundreds of schools in the United States and Canada.

Natural Helpers doesn't train students to be therapists. Instead, it trains them to help each other think through everyday problems like a broken romance or a verbal fight with parents. For major problems like drug dependency, abuse, depression, and suicidal thoughts and feelings, the teen helpers refer their peers to appropriate community resources.

Natural Helpers recruits a variety of students, not just the school leaders. By training students with different learning skills and out-of-school interests, Natural Helpers can be in touch with more kids in trouble.

Natural Helpers believes that teen helpers should not try to solve major problems on their own. They are trained to find a skilled adult and to use three important words: "I need help." Teen helpers also are taught self-help skills so they can take care of themselves while they are helping others.

If you'd like more information about Natural Helpers, write or call:

Comprehensive Health Education Foundation
22323 Pacific Highway South
Seattle, WA 98198
Telephone: (206) 824-2907.

• •

THINGS TO THINK ABOUT AND DO

1. If a friend told you that he or she was going to commit suicide, who would you tell? Can you think of one or more adults who would know what to do? Do you know how to get in touch with these people? Could you reach them at home if you needed to?

2. Would you tell your parents about your friend's suicidal thoughts? Why or why not?

3. Would your parents listen to what you're feeling about your friend's troubles? Why do you think they would or wouldn't listen?

4. No matter how you answered questions 2 and 3, go to your parents and ask them if they would be willing to help you help one of your friends through a suicidal crisis.

5. Find out which adults in your school, such as counselors, teachers, administrators, or the school nurse, are trained in teen suicide prevention. Learn how to get in touch with them. Is there anyone who is available around the clock? If your school publishes a school directory, check to see if the telephone numbers of these trained adults are listed.

6. Find out if your community has an emergency hotline. Write the telephone number on the Important Information form found on page 8 of this book.

• •

SOURCE FOR THE FACTS AND FINDINGS
IN THIS CHAPTER

1. Crook, Marion, *Please, Listen to Me! Your Guide to Understanding Teenagers and Suicide.* Bellingham, WA: Self-Counsel Press, 1992.

How to Help a Friend through a Suicidal Crisis

DO:

- Reach out
- Ask questions
- Show that you care
- Encourage your friend to talk
- Listen without making judgments
- Talk openly about suicide
- Remain calm
- Be positive
- Suggest people you can both turn to
- Know your limits
- Get help
- Act quickly if you think your friend is in danger

DON'T:

- Make your friend's problem sound unimportant
- Act shocked
- Keep your friend's suicide plans secret
- Ask your friend to think about how his or her suicide would make others feel
- Try to take any weapon away from your friend
- Leave your friend alone when he or she is in crisis
- Give up hope

CHAPTER
· 8 ·

HELP YOURSELF

Teen suicide affects more than just the young person who attempts or commits suicide. It affects the helpers—the friends, family members, counselors, teachers, and other concerned, caring persons who try to help the young person work through his or her problems. It affects the survivors—the family members and friends who have lost a loved one to suicide. One teen's suicide also affects other troubled teens who may have been thinking about suicide as an escape from life's problems. The suicide of a classmate, relative, or neighbor may make them decide to act on their own suicidal thoughts.

Someday you may find yourself in one or more of these groups: a friend or relative of a suicide victim, or a troubled teen. Maybe you already are or have been in one of these groups. Doing something about teen suicide means more than helping a friend through a suicidal crisis. It also means knowing how to help yourself—whether you're a helper, a survivor, or a teen who might be thinking about suicide.

Help for Helpers

If You Help a Friend Who Is Thinking about Suicide

Talking to a suicidal friend and going for help can be frightening. It can demand all your energy and concentration and leave you feeling exhausted and confused. Even after your friend is safe and getting help, you may still wonder if you did the right thing. You may worry about how quickly your friend will heal inside. Life may suddenly feel too uncertain, too hard, or too scary.

Your parents may be the best people to share this experience with. Try talking to them even if you think they might not understand everything you went through with your friend. If you can't talk to your parents, find other adults who care about you. Find someone who will listen to you talk about what you went through and how you feel.

You need to hear someone say, "I'm proud of you," because you have, in fact, done something that should make you feel proud. Listen to and accept your listener's praise and positive comments. Stop yourself from saying things like "I didn't do much," "It was no big deal," or "I just did what anyone would do."

You may need to talk about your friend's suicidal crisis more than once. Sometimes telling and retelling your important stories can help you heal.

Your friend's suicidal crisis also may bring up thoughts and feelings inside of you about death and suicide. Don't try to handle these feelings alone. Talk to someone who cares about you.

If Your Friend Attempts Suicide

Don't blame yourself if your friend attempts suicide in spite of your caring, listening, and best efforts to get help. Sometimes nothing you can do or say will change a friend's mind or behavior. You aren't responsible for someone else's life. Repeat to yourself: *The best I can do is the best I can do.*

Your friend's suicide attempt may leave you hurt and confused. You might ask yourself all kinds of questions: "Why would she attempt suicide right after we talked?" "Was it something I said?" "Was it something I didn't say?" "Why did he tell me he was feeling okay and then try to kill himself the next day?" "Did I miss an important warning sign?" "Was I not paying attention?" You might not be able to come up with any answers that make sense to you.

You must believe and remember that your friend did not attempt suicide because of something you said or didn't say. Your friend did not attempt suicide because of something you did or didn't do. Your friend attempted suicide for reasons that had nothing to do with you.

The severity of your friend's emotional pain may have made it impossible for him or her to hear or accept help from anyone. Your friend's stress and pain may have been building for weeks or longer. It may take more than one caring, listening friend to reverse problems that have caused weeks or months of misery.

Special Problems

Sometimes young people have problems that go much deeper than their need to solve a personal crisis. Sometimes young people attempt suicide because they have emotional problems that affect how they interact with others. Let's take a look at some of those possible problems.

People who are chronically suicidal

A few people attempt suicide over and over again. These chronically suicidal individuals will keep trying until they finally kill themselves. They are obsessed with suicide and often resist help.

Blackmailers

Some teens use the threat of suicide as a way to get what they want. Sometimes they want control over the adults in their lives. They might threaten suicide as a way to keep their parents from punishing them or telling them what to do: "If you ground me, I'll kill myself."

Some teens use their past suicide attempts to blackmail people into not expecting too much from them: "If you give me an 'F' in this class, I'll be so upset I'll try and kill myself." "You know I'm suicidal. If I don't make the team, there's no telling what I'll do."

Frequently these young people use suicide threats in an effort to keep romantic relationships from ending: "If you break up with me, I'll kill myself." Their girlfriends or boyfriends feel trapped and responsible, especially if the blackmailer attempts or commits suicide. But they are not responsible for someone who uses blackmail as a way to control other people. If they break up anyway and their blackmailer attempts or commits suicide, they may feel as if they are to blame, but they are not.

Most suicidal teens are looking for a way to end their own pain, but blackmailers want to cause pain for other people. These young people have unhealthy ideas about relationships. They want to control people. Blackmailers make up only a small number of the teens who attempt or commit suicide.

Revenge seekers

Like blackmailers, teens who attempt suicide out of revenge want to hurt someone else. They are not trying to solve a personal problem. Instead, they want to even the score with someone they feel has hurt or offended them.

These teens are irrational. They often become enraged over minor issues or petty arguments. Frequently they are trying to get back at a parent or another adult who they believe has insulted or hurt them. Like blackmailers, revenge seekers need professional help before they can stop using suicide threats to control other people.

Keep Being a Friend

What do you do if your friend is obsessed with suicide or uses a suicide threat as a club to get his or her way? You listen to your friend and you go to an adult for help. If you've done those two things, you've done the best you can. You are not responsible if your friend attempts suicide. Repeat to yourself: *My friend's suicide attempt is not my fault.*

Finally, don't be surprised if you feel angry or disappointed in your friend for attempting suicide. You might feel as if your hard work and listening were all for nothing. It might help to remind yourself that your friend couldn't think of you when he was attempting suicide. His emotions and pain made it impossible for him to think about anything but how he was feeling. Unlike a blackmailer or a revenge seeker, he didn't want to make you angry or disappointed.

Young people who attempt suicide need friends:

- who will continue to be their friends
- who will continue to listen to them
- who will continue to help them
- who will accept them as they are.

Keep being a friend. That's the best—and the most—you can do for anyone.

Help for Survivors

The National Center for Health Statistics estimates that every suicide intimately affects at least six other people, usually the family and closest friends of the young person who committed suicide. This number grows much higher when you include classmates, team members, neighbors, and extended family—aunts, uncles, cousins.

Using the National Center's figures, the American Association of Suicidology estimates that there are more than 4 million suicide survivors in the United States. Each one of them has felt the pain of losing someone they loved.

If you lose a friend to suicide, you'll feel a mixture of emotions. Some of those emotions may surprise you. Some will be difficult for you to understand. Some will last only a few hours or days; others may last months, years, or a lifetime. More than likely, you will go through several stages of grief. These stages—*denial, depression, anger, bargaining,* and *acceptance*—were first clearly explained by Swiss psychiatrist Elisabeth Kübler-Ross. She identified these stages after her years of experience with dying patients and their families.

No one goes through these stages in exactly the same way. Some people may skip a stage altogether, and others may return to one or more of the stages many times. Just as no two people are exactly alike, no two people work through their grief in exactly the same way. But most people will spend some time in each of these stages. Following are descriptions of what you might feel and suggestions for what you can do to help yourself.*

Denial

When you first hear that a friend has committed suicide, you may deny it has happened. Even if you know in your mind that your friend has died, you may deny it in your heart. The death may seem like a bad dream.

To keep from feeling the truth, you may stay away from places and people that remind you of your friend and the suicide. You may stop doing things you did with your friend or listening to the music you both enjoyed. You may get angry at others when they mention the suicide or your friend's name. You may even give away gifts, photos, or mementos that remind you of your friend.

Suggestions

- Find someone you can talk to and just try saying something as brief as "I miss my friend." This short statement will help you get in touch with your feelings of loss.

- Tell someone about something you and your friend did together. Maybe you can remember a story about something funny your friend did or said. Telling these stories will help you to do two things. First, it will help you to accept that your friend really has died. Second, it will help you to remember the things you loved about your friend, the things that made this friend special.

---

*You may also go through these stages of grief if your friend has attempted suicide. Because your friend survived his attempt, you'll probably travel through these stages more quickly than if he actually completed the suicide.

- Hold on to the mementos that remind you of your friend, and put them in a place where you won't have to see them until you feel better.

Depression

Deep sadness or depression is a major stage of grief. During this stage, many people don't want to talk to anyone, and they feel like they have little energy to do anything. They want to be alone. Withdrawing, however, is one of the worst things you can do, because it will make you feel even sadder and lonelier.

Suggestions

Depression, that feeling that makes you feel blue and closed up inside, is the opposite of expression, which is an opening up of feelings and actions. So, one way to ease depression is to find some way to be active and to express your feelings.

- Being with other people can be a helpful first step toward feeling better. Instead of staying alone in your room or avoiding people at school, find someone you can do something with. Just making plans to meet in the school cafeteria to have lunch will give you a place to be and someone to be with.

- Finding ways to help others through their grief will help you feel less sad. You may want to write a note to your friend's parents and tell them why their child was special to you. Others in your school or community also will be grieving. Taking time to listen to their feelings will help you deal with your own.

- Talking is a natural way for people to express themselves. You don't have to talk about the suicide if you don't want to. Just being with someone and talking about anything will help you feel less lonely. But if you know someone you can open up to— your parents, a teacher, a close friend—then telling and retelling the story about your friend, or the suicide and how it made you feel, will help lift your depression.

- Talking isn't the only way to express yourself. If you're a musician, picking up your instrument again will help you to heal. People who are artistic can work out their feelings through their art, and people who enjoy writing can fill pages with their thoughts. Keeping a journal will help get your feelings out. Rereading your journal in the future will remind you that you once had these feelings and show you how, over time, you worked through them.

- Physical activity is a great way to let your body work off its depression. Jogging, walking, swimming—any physical activity that uses your muscles and makes you feel pleasantly tired— will help you feel better.

Anger

Don't be surprised if you feel angry at your friend: "How could you kill yourself?" You may feel angry at yourself: "How could I let this happen?" You may feel angry at the adults in your life: "Why didn't you save him?" You may feel angry at everyone and everything that ever stressed your friend: teachers, parents, a former boss, a girl-friend or boyfriend, last year's broken leg, a dented bumper, even a missed jump shot. You may see them as somehow "betraying" your friend and pushing him or her to commit suicide.

Suggestions

- One way to channel your anger is to get together with others and talk about ways in which your school or community can keep another teen suicide from happening. You'll find ideas in Chapter 9.
- Follow the suggestions for working through the denial stage. They will help you deal with your anger, too.
- Talking, being physically active, and doing the things you once enjoyed also will help you get rid of the anger inside.

Bargaining

Wanting to deny your friend's suicide and wanting to blame your-self for the death play a part in your wish to bargain with fate for another chance. You may wish you could reverse the terrible thing that has happened: "If only my friend could have one more chance. If only I could have one more chance to spot the warning signs, to be a better listener, to get help faster."

These thoughts are natural. The survivors of a suicide often wonder if they couldn't have prevented the suicide, even when it isn't reasonable for them to feel responsible.

Suggestions

Before you can accept your friend's death, you must know in your heart that your friend does not have a second chance. You must believe you were in no way responsible for the death.

- Repeat to yourself: *I did the best that I could. I am not responsible for my friend's death.*

- Talking to others about your feelings of self-blame, and how you wish you and your friend could have another chance, will help you work through this stage.

- You may have questions about your friend's suicide: "How did she die?" "Who saw her last?" "Who found him?" "Did he leave a note?" Finding answers to these questions may help you through this stage. If you know your friend's parents and feel comfortable talking to them, you might ask them for the answers to your questions. They also might need to talk about their child with someone who knew him or her. Your parents or school counselor also may have the answers you need before you can move on to the last stage of grieving.

Acceptance

One day you'll accept that your friend has died. On that day you will have passed through the final stage of grief. You won't feel happy about the death, but you'll be able to live with the fact that it happened.

Suggestions

- Don't be afraid to talk about your friend or to remember things you did together.

- If you hid any mementos, go find them and put them out in your room or in an album.

Once you've passed through the stages of grief, talking about or remembering the person who has died won't start your grieving all over again. You may still have moments when you cry or feel like crying. That's okay. Missing someone who has gone away is natural and healthy. It is a reminder that your friend was special.

• •

WAYS TO WORK THROUGH YOUR GRIEF

- Tell yourself that feeling sad is normal.
- Cry when you need to.
- Spend time with family and friends.
- Do things you enjoy.
- Stay active.
- Talk or write about your feelings.
- Find ways to help others.
- Join with others and come up with ideas on how to stop teen suicide.
- Put your ideas into action.

• •

Protect Yourself against Suicide

You have been learning about suicide and ways to help other people who may be thinking about suicide. But don't forget to help and protect another important person in your life: you.

Do you remember the weights and balloons we described in Chapter 1? Negative things in your life can feel like 100-pound weights around your neck. Positive things can feel like powerful balloons that balance the weights in your life.

Take a few moments to think about how many weights and balloons you have in your life. How are you feeling right now? Are you carrying too many weights? Are there enough balloons to balance your weights and to keep your self-concept high? Doing the Self-Check will give you some answers.

• •

SELF-CHECK: ARE YOUR WEIGHTS AND BALLOONS IN BALANCE?

1. On a separate sheet of paper, list all the things that made you feel good last week. Don't forget to include things you might take for granted, such as listening to a great CD, getting a hug from your mom or dad, or riding your bike in the sunshine. These are your *balloons.*

2. Now list all the things that happened last week that made you feel emotions like anger, embarrassment, frustration, sadness, or fear. These are your *weights.*

3. Compare your lists. Is one much longer than the other? What does that tell you about the balance of balloons and weights in your life?

4. Look at your list of weights again and answer these questions:

   • Which ones have gone away since last week?

   • Which ones still make you feel weighted down?

   • Which ones can you make better by yourself?

   • Which ones require you to have help?

• •

Are you generally happy at school, in your home, on the job, on the athletic field? Do you usually get along with your family, friends, teachers and coaches? Do you feel good about yourself most of the time? Do you feel as if there are many things you can do well? Do you feel relaxed, or are you tight and tense inside? Do you often feel like you do when you're getting ready to take an important test or give a speech in front of the class?

It's okay if you decide you're a little stressed out now and then or if you know you have some problems. Your life will always have some stress and problems. Even if they don't always feel positive, a certain amount of problem-solving and stress is good for you.

For example, solving the problem of how to balance the demands of a part-time job and full-time school work may be hard. But when you figure out how you'll do both, you'll have learned skills that will help you throughout life.

Deciding how you'll resist peer pressure to try drinking or sex before you feel ready is never easy. But learning how to be your own person will give you a lifetime of self-confidence.

You already solve many problems every day. You decide things like what to wear to school, how to study for your history test, how to ask your boss for a day off, and how to save money for the new jeans you want to buy. These problems certainly aren't as serious as deciding how you'll say "no" to peer pressure, but most problems, big or small, can be solved by following some basic steps.

• •

SIX-STEP PROBLEM-SOLVING

Imagine that you've got a problem: what to do on Friday night. Here are six steps that can lead you toward a solution.

STEP 1: *Define the problem.*

I have to decide what I'm doing Friday night.

STEP 2: *List the alternatives as you see them.*

I could:

- stay home and watch TV
- go over to Bill's
- go to the movies with Janet

STEP 3: *List sources of help or other information.*

- Ask Mom about using the car on Friday. ("Okay," she says, "but only if you help me clean house in time for Sunday's company dinner at 2 p.m. Oh, and I expect you to be home for dinner on Sunday.")
- Call Bill. ("I won't be home Friday night," he says. "How about Sunday?")
- Call Janet. ("I have to work Friday night," she says. "Can we go to a movie on Saturday?")

STEP 4: *List your alternatives as you now understand* them.

On Friday, I could:

- stay home and watch TV (old idea)
- clean house (Mom's idea) and ask to use the car on Saturday and Sunday

STEP 5: *Think through your options.*

- If I want the car, I have to clean house Friday night or Saturday
- If I want to see Janet, it has to be on Saturday
- If I can't see Bill on Friday, I can see him on Sunday
- If I do anything on Sunday, it has to be after dinner

STEP 6: *Take action.*

- Get the vacuum and dust rags out on Friday
- Pick up Janet on Saturday
- Drop by Bill's on Sunday after 4 p.m.

• •

Just as problem-solving can be helpful, stress can also have some benefits. In fact, not all stress is bad, and some good things can cause stress. Family vacations are fun but stressful. The holidays are happy but stressful. Getting a new job, even one you really want, can be stressful.

Stress can also work as a motivator. Many athletes perform at their peak when they're stressed and trying to come from behind. Many entertainers give their best performances when they're stressed. Many students write their best papers or exams when they're stressed.

Although some amount of stress and problem-solving can be good, too much stress can be dangerous. Having to solve problems that are too big for you to handle alone—such as a pregnancy, an alcoholic parent, or emotional, physical, or sexual abuse—can dangerously add to your stress levels and make you physically or emotionally ill. As you learned in Chapters 1 and 4, having more weights than balloons and having problems that are too big to solve can put some teens at risk for suicide.

How do you know when you're suffering from too much stress? Your body will give you some of the best clues. You may have one or more of these symptoms:

- frequent headaches and stomach aches
- a sudden attack of asthma
- difficulty concentrating, sleeping, eating, or breathing
- frequent outbursts of temper, tears, and irritability.

When you're stressed enough to show these symptoms, you may not make wise or reasonable decisions. You may start to feel negative about your environments and the people in your life. You might withdraw to get away from everything and everyone that annoys you. If you withdraw, you run the risk of becoming deeply depressed. This cycle of stress, annoyance, withdrawal, and deep sadness can sometimes lead to thoughts of suicide.

Help for When You're Feeling Stressed

An important way you can protect yourself against suicide is to pay attention to your stress levels, to how you feel inside, and to what causes you to feel stressed. If you start to show or feel the emotional or physical symptoms of too much stress, find someone you can talk to. Tell them about these feelings and symptoms and when and how often they happen. You also can do some things to ease the stress in your life.

- You'll feel less stressed naturally if you get enough rest, eat balanced meals, and keep healthy and fit.
- Balance the stressful parts of your life with activities and interests that are less stressful. If you're a serious student, take a break and do something that isn't mentally taxing. If you're a competitive athlete, include another activity in your life that doesn't require you to compete.
- Work off your stress by doing something physical. Run, mow the lawn, dance, lift weights, do calisthenics, or take a brisk walk.
- Talk out your stress. Find someone you trust and feel comfortable confiding in.

- Do something for others. Tutor younger school children, volunteer at a local hospital, make regular visits to a person who lives in a nursing home, tell your parents you'll cook dinner, or offer to drive your little sister to soccer practice.

- Give yourself permission to make mistakes and to admit them. You don't always have to be perfect.

- Remind yourself that you don't have to solve the world's problems today. You don't have to decide your whole future this minute. One bad day doesn't mean that only bad days will follow.

- Set aside time to dream. To jump-start your imagination, try drawing or writing in a journal.

- Keep life interesting. Try something new now and then. Make new friends, eat new foods, try a different hairstyle, or find a new hobby.

- Identify the sources of your stress. Then ask yourself, "Is there anything I can do to reduce the stress in my life? Can I cut out or change any of the sources of my stress?"

On page 101, you'll find a list of events and situations that are known to stress young people. Many of these items can cause negative or bad stress, and many of these stressors have happened to young people who attempted suicide. Some of these items are positive things that can bring good stress.

Those items at or near the top of the list most often can be heavy sources of stress. Those at or near the bottom are lighter sources of stress.

Check off all the items that have happened to you in the last six months. Then look at your list. Do you have a lot of check marks near the top half of the list? How many checks do you have between items 1 and 20? If you have more than five checks between these numbers, you probably are under a great deal of stress. Find an adult you trust and show him or her your list. Together you can decide if you need to talk to a counselor.

What if most of your checks are between items 21 and 40? If you have 10 or more checks after item 20, show your list to an adult you trust and talk about the things that have been happening in your life.

Checking things off on this list and then looking at where the checks fall will give you clues about the amount of stress you might be feeling. Having fewer than five checks in the first half of the list or less than ten in the last half isn't a guarantee that you aren't feeling too much stress. Use this list simply as a guide to thinking about the stress in your life. Don't ignore how you are feeling inside and any physical symptoms of stress you may be experiencing.

TIP: If you're worried that a friend seems stressed or down, check off the items on this list that you know have happened to your friend. Then show the list to your friend and see if he or she can add any more checks. The list might help your friend open up to you.

• •

Crisis Checklist

1. __ Parent dies
2. __ Parents get divorced
3. __ Parents separate
4. __ A friend or relative commits suicide
5. __ You abuse alcohol or other drugs
6. __ You break up with your boyfriend or girlfriend
7. __ Physical or sexual abuse occurs in the home
8. __ A friend or relative attempts suicide
9. __ Someone you love dies of natural causes
10. __ Family member abuses alcohol or other drugs
11. __ You are gay, lesbian, or questioning your sexual orientation
12. __ Emotional abuse occurs in the home
13. __ You become pregnant
14. __ You suffer a major illness or injury
15. __ You have problems with your school work
16. __ Violence happens in your school
17. __ You learn your girlfriend is pregnant
18. __ You move to a new city
19. __ You have difficulty getting along with your friends
20. __ You start at a new school or get a new teacher
21. __ A new baby sister or brother arrives
22. __ A family member becomes ill or injured
23. __ Parent is fired
24. __ Mother goes to work full time
25. __ Home is burned or robbed
26. __ You fight with brothers and sisters
27. __ Your family has money problems
28. __ Your pet dies or gets lost
29. __ You start a new sport or other activity
30. __ Your sleeping habits change
31. __ Violence happens in your neighborhood
32. __ Family member moves away
33. __ You get a new job
34. __ You win an award
35. __ You fight with grandparents
36. __ Family goes on vacation
37. __ You go to summer camp
38. __ You apply to college
39. __ Your amount of TV watching changes
40. __ The family celebrates a birthday or holiday

• ● • • • • • • • • • • • • • • • • • • •

●●

ASK YOURSELF...

As one last check-up on how you're feeling, ask yourself these questions:

- Do I feel like a failure?
- Am I lonely?
- Do I lack self-confidence?
- Do I have a low opinion of myself?
- Do I think about suicide?

If you answered "yes" to the last question and at least three others, go *right away* to an adult you trust and feel comfortable talking to. Show him or her these questions and tell how you answered them. Ask the adult to help you. Don't stop asking until you get the help you need.

●●

Books That Can Help You to Help Yourself

Sometimes the right book can pick up your spirits and get you thinking about new and positive things. Following are some suggestions you may want to check out. Ask your teacher or librarian for other recommendations.

- *Please, Listen to Me! Your Guide to Understanding Teenagers and Suicide* by Marion Crook (Self-Counsel Press, 1992) is written for parents to help them understand why their child might think about or attempt suicide and what they can do to help a troubled child. But this easy-to-read, easy-to-understand book will also give you insights into why teen suicide happens. It will help you to understand why teen suicide is so frightening to parents and what parents must do to overcome their fears and to reach out to their children.

- *Fighting Invisible Tigers: A Stress Management Guide for Teens* by Earl Hipp (Free Spirit Publishing, 1985) includes strategies for surviving and thriving in the "jungle of life."

- *Making the Most of Today: Daily Readings for Young People on Self-Awareness, Creativity, and Self-Esteem* by Pamela Espeland and Rosemary Wallner (Free Spirit Publishing, 1991) is a year's worth of positive thinking, problem solving, and practical lifeskills to help you know yourself better, be more creative, and feel better about yourself.

- *Stick Up for Yourself! Every Kid's Guide to Personal Power and Positive Self-Esteem* by Gershen Kaufman and Lev Raphael (Free Spirit Publishing, 1990) is packed with ideas about how you can feel good about yourself. Written for ages 8 to 12, it's meaningful for all ages.

- *When a Friend Dies: A Book for Teens about Grieving and Healing* by Marilyn E. Gootman (Free Spirit Publishing, 1994) offers genuine understanding and gentle advice for any teen who is grieving the death of a friend.

CHAPTER
· 9 ·

GET YOUR SCHOOL
AND COMMUNITY
INVOLVED

The best place to start a teen suicide prevention program is with young people like you and your friends. About 90 percent of the junior high and high school students who think about suicide first share their thoughts with a friend. So teens know how other teens feel, and they hear each others' problems.

Most teens begin to think seriously about suicide prevention after a friend has attempted or committed suicide. After their friend's crisis, they may feel guilty: "Did I do enough to help my friend?" They may feel angry: "Why did my friend do that?" They may also feel helpless: "Why didn't someone do something?" Often these feelings and the desire to do something about teen suicide get teens thinking. Often these young people meet with other students and adults in their schools and communities to talk about the teen suicide problem.

Many schools and communities have started teen suicide prevention programs after one or more teens in their area committed suicide. Plano and Laredo in Texas, Jefferson County in Colorado, the Shawnee Mission School District in Overland Park, Kansas, and Omaha, Nebraska, are among the many places where suicide programs were begun in direct response to an outbreak of teen suicides.

Young people already are working hard for many good causes: hunger, homelessness, illiteracy, and a cleaner, safer Earth. Many join Students Against Driving Drunk (SADD) and work to keep teens from drinking, driving, and dying in their cars. Many have signed up with the "Just Say No" campaign because they know drugs destroy lives.

National organizations like SADD and "Just Say No" show that young people can come together to reduce or solve the problems that harm them and their friends.

• •

PROOF THAT YOUNG PEOPLE
CAN MAKE A DIFFERENCE

Kids with Courage: True Stories about Young People Making a Difference by Barbara Lewis (Free Spirit Publishing, 1992) is filled with real-life examples of young people who have improved others' lives. Like Charles Carson, 19, of Tacoma, Washington, who started a program to fight teen violence, drugs, and crime. And Mercedes Jones, 16, of Louisville, Kentucky, who started a program to make others aware of sexual abuse. They and other teens profiled in this book all experienced traumas they didn't want other young people to go through. They decided to do something. Their efforts and successes prove that young people can make a difference.

....

Who Needs to Know about Teen Suicide?

You don't have to wait until someone in your school attempts or commits suicide. Right now, in your school and community, young people are thinking about suicide.

There are four groups in your area that urgently need suicide information and education:

- *Teenagers:* Most young people have not received enough information about teen suicide. After reading this book, you know more about teen suicide than many people do, including adults.

- *Parents:* Like their sons and daughters, most parents know little about suicide. Many are afraid of suicide. They believe that suicide is what happens to "other people's children." Parents also fear that if their son or daughter is suicidal, it must mean they have done a bad job as parents. Sometimes they have, but more often they haven't. Parents need to know more about teen suicide, and they need to become involved in finding solutions to the problem.

- *School staff:* Teachers, counselors, nurses, custodians, cooks, bus drivers, and principals all come in contact with young people who are thinking about suicide. All of these people need information about teen suicide so they can spot and get help for a young person who is suicidal.

- *Community groups:* Civic groups, youth organizations, churches, temples, and local businesses all need suicide information. These groups often have the resources to help support important projects. Sometimes they can contribute money, and often they can find volunteers who will get involved.

How You Can Educate Others: A Step-by-Step Action Plan

If you'd like to start a project to educate others and help prevent teen suicide in your area, follow these steps.

1. *Invite one or more friends to help you.* Having someone to think and plan with will get more ideas flowing. Friends support each other and keep each other motivated.

2. *Define the problem.* How many young people in your community have attempted suicide in the past two years? How many committed suicide during that time? The counselors and principals in your community's schools can help you with these numbers.

3. *Learn as much as you can about suicide.* Look in magazines and newspapers for current information, and read books. Your librarian can help you locate materials. Call or write to organizations that have suicide programs and find out what they're doing and what they have learned. Talk to other young people about their experiences with suicide. Talk to teachers and parents to get their ideas. Call schools in your area and see what they've done; they might have ideas you can borrow or improve on.

   In Kansas, for example, a third of all the schools give students in grades 7 through 12 information about teen suicide. Students learn about the warning signs and about the myths surrounding suicide. They also learn what to do for themselves or for friends to prevent suicide. Most often these lessons are taught as part of ninth-grade health classes.

4. *Find out what, if anything, is already being done to educate people in your community about teen suicide.* Learn if other groups are already working to prevent teen suicide and what they are doing. Don't spend days or weeks developing your project only to discover that another group or organization already has a program up and running. Suicide is a big problem, so there's more than enough work for everyone who wants to get involved. Some places to start and questions to ask are:

- Do people in your school and community have access to up-to-date information about suicide? See what books about suicide are available in your school and public libraries. Are they current?

- Does your school offer programs about teen suicide? These programs are most often presented in health class, special courses, and after-school groups. Find out if there are any age limitations. Are the programs only for high school students? You may want to propose a program for junior high/middle school students—even grade school students.

- Do religious youth groups in your area teach young people about suicide? Are their programs for anyone or for members only?

- Do your local scout or 4-H groups have teen suicide programs?

If you find a good program that already exists, get involved. If you don't, go on to the next step.

5. *Brainstorm many plans and possible solutions to the problem of educating others about teen suicide.* Don't only look for the one best approach. Be creative, even silly; some great ideas have come from off-the-wall suggestions.

6. *Build a strong support team.* It's natural to want to own and protect your ideas. Suicide, however, is a problem that touches many peoples' lives, and to succeed you'll need the help of everyone who supports what you're doing. Parents, the school staff, community leaders, and other young people will help make your project come to life.

Check with your local Junior Chamber of Commerce, Optimists Clubs, and Lions Clubs. Many sponsor youth projects in their communities. Some civic groups might be interested in working with students to promote a suicide education and prevention program in your area.

7. *Develop your plan.* Decide exactly what you want to do. Here are some questions you might ask:

- What do young people need to know about suicide?
- How can they get that information?
- What does the school staff need to know about suicide?

- How can they become better informed?
- What can be done to involve community groups?

Based on your answers, develop a goal for your plan. For example, you might decide that you want to start a 24-hour crisis hotline at your school. Developing a sound plan and having a clear goal will help you succeed.

8. *Be prepared for the opposition.* Many people believe that talking about suicide increases the number of suicides. That belief is incorrect, but you'll probably meet some people who will use that misconception to oppose your efforts. If you've done your research, you can respond to their objections, arguments, and fears. If adults with influence—such as your principal, school board members, and other elected officials, parents or business leaders—support your project, they'll help you work around any resistance.

9. *Contact the media.* The media should be involved for two reasons. First, your local radio and television stations and newspaper will want to let others know what you're doing. The stories they produce will be great advertising for your project. Second, media people need to be educated about suicide.

Many studies have shown that detailed and dramatic coverage of suicides increases the number of suicides in an area. Newspaper, television, and radio reporters who sensationalize a suicide story send the message that suicide is an acceptable way to attract attention.

Stories about suicide should do two things: they should report only the facts, and they should also mention places in the community where troubled teens can get help. In this way the media can do the job of covering the news and also provide a valuable service.

10. *Start your project.* If you've involved a lot of people in your project, getting started should be fun.

11. *After a reasonable period of time, evaluate your project.*

- Is it doing what you want it to do?
- How do students feel about it?
- What do parents and the school staff say about it?
- How has the community responded?

- Are you pleased with the project's progress?
- Can you list some positive things that have happened because of your project? Some negative things?

Keep and improve the things that are working. Eliminate or improve the things that aren't.

Starting a teen suicide education and prevention program may seem like a huge task, but don't give up. Many young people have tackled problems just as big, and they have succeeded. So will you. Remember, you don't have to solve the teen suicide problem alone. You don't have to start the program by yourself. Other people in your community, school, and family will help. Together you can all do something to save young people from taking their own lives.

Teens who attempt or commit suicide are choosing not to live. When young people have other choices, fewer will choose suicide. Suicide education and prevention programs give young people other choices.

• •

IF YOU WANT TO KNOW MORE....

For more tips, ideas, and advice on how you can get together with other young people to work on a problem such as teen suicide, read *The Kid's Guide to Social Action: How to Solve the Social Problems You Choose—And Turn Creative Thinking into Positive Action* by Barbara Lewis (Free Spirit Publishing, 1991). This book includes many true stories about young people who wrote letters and proposals, visited their legislatures, contacted the media, and wrote grant proposals so they could solve problems that were important to them. You'll find letters, proposals, interview forms, and more ready for you to copy and use, plus step-by-step directions.

• •

A National Group against Youth Suicide

Young people working with SADD and "Just Say No" have helped save young lives by discouraging drinking and driving. What would happen if students formed a group against youth suicide? We believe this group could also save young people's lives.

We're inviting you to start a chapter of Students Preventing Youth Suicide—SPYS—in your school or community. Like real spies, members of SPYS would look for the clues that reveal when a young person might be in danger of suicide. Like real spies, members of SPYS would pass along what they know about suicide and about their troubled classmates to the adults trained to help these young people.

At the time this book is being published, a national network of information and programs on teen suicide prevention is only an idea. But we believe that young people across the country can make it a reality.

Would you be interested in organizing a SPYS group in your school or youth group? If your answer is "yes," please write or call:

Dr. Richard E. Nelson, Assistant Director
Counseling and Psychological Services
Watkins Health Center
The University of Kansas
Lawrence, KS 66045
Telephone: (913) 864-2277.

Copy this page, cut out the card, fold it, and tuck it in your wallet. Carry it with you at all times. *Idea:* Maybe a civic organization in your community would adopt the project of printing and distributing this card as its project to prevent youth suicide.

Find an adult you trust and say,
"I NEED HELP."
OR call 911 or "0" for operator.

Friend	_____	Phone # _____
Clergy	_____	Phone # _____
Counselor	_____	Phone # _____
Crisis Line	_____	Phone # _____

Suicide Warning Signs

- Depression
- Sudden changes in behavior
- Suicide threats
- Broken romance, death in the family— any significant personal loss
- Aggression, rebelliousness, disobedience
- Giving away treasured possessions
- Suicide threats
- Self-destructive behavior

PART THREE

....

RESOURCES

Crisis Assistance

Communities throughout the United States and Canada have emergency crisis centers with phones that often are answered around the clock. To find the phone number of the crisis center nearest you, look in the white pages or Yellow Pages of your phone book under "Suicide," "Suicide Prevention," or "Suicide Hotline." If you need to talk to someone right now and can't find the number of your local crisis center, call one of the three national hotlines listed below.

Covenant House Nineline
1-800-999-9999
24 hours, 7 days a week

Covenant House, located in New York City, has a nationwide phone line to take calls from young people in trouble. The program primarily works with homeless youth who have run away or who have been abandoned, but it also helps young people who are suicidal. The phone worker can give you immediate crisis intervention or can use Nineline's listing of more than 24,000 agencies to find the crisis center nearest you.

Boys Town National Hotline
1-800-448-3000
1-800-448-1833 (hearing impaired)
24 hours, 7 days a week

Located in Nebraska, this hotline can be reached from all 50 states, Canada, Puerto Rico, and the Virgin Islands. Its trained counselors talk to more than 500,000 troubled and suicidal teens each year. The hotline's staff includes Spanish-speaking operators. A TTY machine also enables counselors to communicate with those who are hearing impaired. Using the hotline's database of more than 50,000 local agencies and services, Boys Town counselors can tell you where to find the crisis center or services nearest you.

Primary Health Management Systems
1-800-444-9999
Daily from 6:30 p.m.–10:30 p.m. Pacific Standard Time

This crisis line for suicidal teenagers is located in southern California, but it takes calls from anywhere in the 50 states and Canada. The line is open from 6:30 p.m. to 10:30 p.m. Pacific Standard Time. The phone worker can give you the number of the crisis intervention center nearest you. Phone workers at this hotline also give on-the-spot support and try to talk suicidal teens out of doing anything dangerous.

A Suicide Crisis Center Directory

The American Association of Suicidology publishes a comprehensive directory of suicide prevention and crisis intervention centers in the 50 states and the District of Columbia, Puerto Rico, and Canada. The 70-page directory includes the agencies' names, addresses, business and crisis phone numbers, and hours of operation.

School counselors, ministers, youth group directors, and the staff at local mental health centers should all know where the closest crisis centers are in your community, state, and region. They would find this directory to be very useful. Please share this information about the directory with the adults in your life.

The directory costs $18.00 per single copy, including postage and handling. To order a copy, write or call:

The American Association of Suicidology
4201 Connecticut Avenue, NW, Suite 310
Washington, D.C. 20008
Telephone: (202) 237-2280
FAX: (202) 237-2282

Readings and References

We wrote *The Power to Prevent Suicide* to tell young people like you how you can help a friend survive his or her suicidal thoughts or plans. Many other books, however, have important things to say about suicide in general and about teen suicide in particular. You may want to read one or more of the following books to learn even more about teen suicide.

- David L. Bender and Bruno Leone, editors, *Suicide: Opposing Viewpoints*. San Diego: Greenhaven Press, 1992.

You'll read a variety of opinions on suicide, from those of the right-to-die supporters to those deeply opposed to suicide. Chapter 3 deals specifically with teen suicide, and the remaining chapters examine the problems and questions about why anyone would choose to die, suicide for the terminally ill, and suicide prevention.

- David B. Bergman, *Kids on the Brink: Understanding the Teen Suicide Epidemic*. Washington, DC: PIA Press, 1990.

This highly readable book weaves dozens of stories about suicidal young people into solid facts and information about teen suicide and its causes.

- Marilyn Gootman, Ed.D., *When a Friend Dies: A Book for Teens about Grieving and Healing*. Minneapolis: Free Spirit Publishing Inc., 1994.

Understanding, gentle advice, and practical suggestions for any teen who is grieving the death of a friend for any reason, including suicide.

- Margaret O. Hyde and Elizabeth Held Forsyth, *Suicide: The Hidden Epidemic*. New York: Franklin Watts, 1978.

This easy-to-read book was among the first to take a serious look at teen suicide. Thorough and helpful, it offers information on the history of suicide, cultural attitudes, and theories on why people want to die.

- Francine Klagsbrun, *Too Young to Die: Youth & Suicide*. New York: Houghton Mifflin, 1976.

This informative book gives a good overview of teen suicide and its issues and includes information on depression and mental illness, plus an extensive bibliography.

- Roxane Brown Kunz and Judy Harris Swenson, *Feeling Down: The Way Back Up*. Minneapolis: Dillon Press, 1986.

Directed at the brothers and sisters of a suicide victim, this book urges open communication between family members. More than many other books on suicide, this one stresses learning how to cope with life's pressures, how to approach therapy, and how to create a nurturing home life.

- John Langone, *Dead End: A Book About Suicide*. New York: Little, Brown, 1986.

Many young people's voices are scattered throughout this informative book. The chapters cover such topics as the right to die, suicide notes, depression, the history of suicide, and 12 tips for befriending a suicidal person. Footnotes and an index make this a good book to read before giving a report on suicide.

- Arnold Madison, *Suicide and Young People*. San Francisco: Seabury Press, 1978.

Written for kids as young as first grade, this simple book gives a good overview of youth suicide. The author includes chapters on suicide among minority children, youth suicides in other countries, and a look at a suicide prevention center.

- Stella Pevsner, *How Could You Do It, Diana?* New York: Clarion, 1989.

In this YA (Young Adult) novel, a younger sister struggles to understand why her sister committed suicide. This true-to-life story takes a thoughtful look at suicide from the feelings of the survivors.

- Mary Q. Steele, *The Life (and Death) of Sarah Elizabeth Harwood*. New York: Greenwillow Books, 1980.

Worried about death and when it will strike her, the 11-year-old heroine decides to jump off a building and just get it all over with. Elizabeth doesn't commit suicide, but she reveals a young person's realistic thoughts about dying and death.

INDEX

About the Authors

Dr. Richard E. Nelson has given more than 600 workshops and seminars in 27 states on suicide prevention, youth at risk, and stress. He has been a high school teacher, a counselor in junior high and high school, and a junior high school principal. He now works at the University of Kansas as the assistant director of Counseling and Psychological Services at Watkins Student Health Center and is an associate professor of counseling psychology. In 1994, Dr. Nelson was the first recipient of the Kansas School Counselor Association award for Outstanding Post-Secondary Counselor in Kansas. In recognition of outstanding service to counseling in Kansas, he was also awarded the Kansas Counseling Association Hall of Fame Award for 1994. He most enjoys spending time with his family: his wife, Barbara, and their two sons, a daughter, and two grandchildren.

Judith C. Galas started as a journalist in 1978 and has reported from Montana, New York, London, and Kansas City. She now works full-time as a free-lance writer and especially enjoys the books she has written for young people. She lives in Lawrence, Kansas, with her partner, Cindy; their daughter, Amy; and Abigail, an Old English sheepdog. An avid walker, she has walked more than a thousand miles in two years with Cindy, and together they write and publish books on walking.

More Books From Free Spirit

When A Friend Dies:
A Book for Teens About Grieving and Healing
by Marilyn Gootman, Ed.D.

Genuine understanding and gentle advice for any teenager who is grieving the death of a friend. This book speaks directly to young people with wisdom, experience, and compassion to help them cope with their sadness and begin to heal. Ages 11 & up.
$7.95; 120 pp; s/c; 5" x 7"

Fighting Invisible Tigers:
A Stress Management Guide for Teens
Revised and Updated Edition
by Earl Hipp

Proven, practical advice for teens on coping with stress, being assertive, building relationships, taking risks, making decisions, dealing with fears, and more. A perennial bestseller. Ages 11 & up.
$10.95; 160 pp; illus.; s/c; 6" x 9"

Leader's Guide
12 Sessions on Stress Management and Lifeskills Development
Revised and Updated Edition
by Connie C. Schmitz, Ph.D., with Earl Hipp

Twelve independent, flexible sessions teach specific stress-management skills. Includes 24 reproducible handout masters. For teachers grades 6–12.
$19.95; 136 pp.; illus.; s/c; 8½" x 11"

Find these books in your favorite bookstore, or contact:

Free Spirit Publishing Inc.
400 First Avenue North • Suite 616 • Minneapolis, MN 55401-1724
toll-free (800) 735-7323 • local (612) 338-2068 • fax (612) 337-5050
www.freespirit.com • help4kids@freespirit.com